INSPIRING AFRICAN AMERICANS
Black History Makers in the United States, 1750–1984

by
George L. Lee

with a foreword by
DR. HELEN E. WILLIAMS

McFarland & Company, Inc., Publishers
Jefferson, North Carolina, and London

920.0092,
L478i

British Library Cataloguing-in-Publication data are available

Library of Congress Cataloguing-in-Publication Data

Lee, George L., 1906–
    Inspiring African Americans : black history makers in the United States,
1750–1984 / by George L. Lee.
      p. cm.
    Includes index.
    ISBN 0-89950-576-7 (lib. bdg. : 55# alk. paper)
    1. Blacks—Biography. 2. Afro-Americans—Biography. I. Title.
CT105.L35 1991
920′009296—dc20
  [B]   90-53503
                                                  CIP

Manufactured in the United States of America

McFarland & Company, Inc., Publishers
  Box 611, Jefferson, North Carolina 28640

1992

JUN.

Inspiring African Americans

Dedicated to
my late wife, Jennie
my son, Richard
my granddaughter, Terri
my late brother, Bill
and my great-granddaughter, Corryn

Foreword

Lives of great men all remind us
We can make our lives sublime,
And, departing, leave behind us
Footprints on the sands of Time.

This stanza from Henry W. Longfellow's "Psalm of Life" (albeit exclusive of women) provides a poetic sketch of the primary purpose of this book. It represents some of the outstanding African American achievers of historical and contemporary times. It is intended for readers and non-readers among the young, their parents, teachers, librarians, and the general public.

Psychologists and youth advocates have long recognized that books and other learning materials which reflect truthfully and positively the culture of the reader also serve to contribute meaningfully to the reader's self-esteem and level of ethnic awareness and pride. This book's emphasis of the positive is intended to present to African American children some image-enhancing information from their ethnic backgrounds. It will also present to other ethnic readers an indigenous perspective toward a deeper and clearer understanding of the contributions of African American people.

The struggle is continuing to dispel derogatory stereotypes of African Americans as well as images of them as perpetual children in need of white parental care and direction. This book contains important stories of persons who have succeeded in spite of prejudice against the color of their skin. Their achievements and determination to succeed position them as desirable role models for all young people, regardless of the reader's ethnicity.

The use potential of this book is exciting because the subjects and contents encourage interaction and sharing, as well as individual perusal. Strategies can easily be developed for parent-child or siblings' memory recall games and quizzes. I am excited that this book is available and I anticipate optimistically its frequent use.

Dr. Helen E. Williams
University of Maryland
1990

v

Contents

Contents

Contents

Preface

My career as a newspaper artist began soon after I arrived in Chicago in 1927. With no formal art education my thinking was school—perhaps a commercial art school. I applied at the Vogue Art School and was politely told that they did not accept Negro students. So I enrolled at the Art Institute, but withdrew when I found I didn't like figure drawing. I had been fascinated by sports drawings in newspapers so I turned to the papers and sports. Much of my initial work involved the sports world and is documented in a recent sports book, *Interesting Athletes* (McFarland, 1990).

The drawings in *Inspiring African Americans* are from my black press feature, "Interesting People," which I created in 1945 and suspended in 1948 due to the shortage of newsprint right after World War II. In 1970 I resumed "Interesting People" after retirement from a 33-year career with the U.S. Postal Service. I continued drawing until 1986 when I retired at the age of 80.

The first collection of this feature in book form was *Interesting People* (McFarland, 1989). This second collection, as with *Interesting People,* is arranged in approximate chronological order according to the life dates of the persons depicted.

This book is intended to provide interesting stories about people of achievement. May each reader find a source of inspiration within these pages.

George L. Lee

ACCORDING TO HISTORIANS

LEMUEL HAYNES 1753 1833

THE SON OF A AFRICAN NATIVE AND A WHITE WOMAN WHO DESERTED HIM AT BIRTH. A NEW ENGLANDER, HE ROSE TO BE A LEADING CONGREGATION- ALIST PREACHER. FAIR-SKINNED HE WAS PROBABLY THE FIRST NEGRO TO PASTOR A WHITE CHURCH IN RUTLAND, VT. HIS ELOQUENCE HAD A LARGE FOLLOWING. DURING THE REVOLUTIONARY WAR HE WAS AMONG SEVERAL NEGRO MINUTE- MEN. HAYNES FOUGHT AT LEXINGTON AND CONCORD BRIDGE (1775). LATER JOINED ETHAN ALLEN AND THE GREEN MOUNTAIN BOYS IN THE CAPTURE OF FORT TICONDEROGA.

Geo Lee

JAMES ARMISTEAD

A VIRGINIA SLAVE WAS THE GREATEST NEGRO SPY DURING THE REVOLU- TIONARY WAR. GENERAL LAFAYETTE NAMED HIM HIS CHIEF SPY. ARMISTEAD HELPED TO TRAP GEN. CORNWALLIS (BRIT). IN 1786 WAS GRANTED FREEDOM FOR HIS HEROISM.

1978 GEO L. LEE FEATURE SERVICE

1

UP FROM SLAVERY

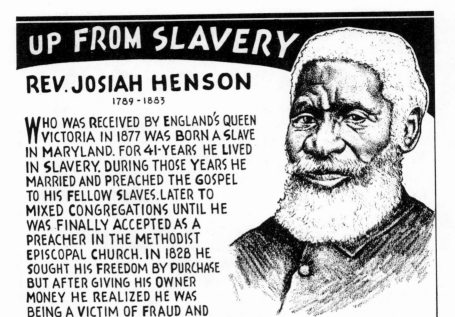

REV. JOSIAH HENSON
1789 - 1883

WHO WAS RECEIVED BY ENGLAND'S QUEEN VICTORIA IN 1877 WAS BORN A SLAVE IN MARYLAND. FOR 41-YEARS HE LIVED IN SLAVERY. DURING THOSE YEARS HE MARRIED AND PREACHED THE GOSPEL TO HIS FELLOW SLAVES. LATER TO MIXED CONGREGATIONS UNTIL HE WAS FINALLY ACCEPTED AS A PREACHER IN THE METHODIST EPISCOPAL CHURCH. IN 1828 HE SOUGHT HIS FREEDOM BY PURCHASE BUT AFTER GIVING HIS OWNER MONEY HE REALIZED HE WAS BEING A VICTIM OF FRAUD AND WAS TO BE SOLD. HE ESCAPED IN 1830

TO UPPER CANADA WITH HIS FAMILY. HE BECAME A LEADER AMONG OTHER FUGITIVE SLAVES. IN 1841 HE ORGANIZED A GROUP OF ABOLITIONISTS AND FOUNDED THE FIRST VOCATIONAL SCHOOL IN CANADA-BRITISH-AMERICAN INSTITUTE FOR FUGITIVE SLAVES NEAR THE NOW TOWN OF DRESDEN, ONT. HARRIET BEECHER STOWE USED HIS LIFE AS A SLAVE IN HER BEST SELLING NOVEL IN 1852 — "UNCLE TOM'S CABIN."

GEO LEE

FIRST BLACK COLLEGE PRESIDENT

1811
1893

BISHOP DANIEL A. PAYNE

NOTED SCHOLAR OF THE A.M.E CHURCH WAS A FREE BLACK OF CHARLESTON, S.C. GIFTED WITH A MIND THAT ABSORBED KNOWLEDGE WITH SURPRISING EASE. HE LEARNED TO READ, WRITE, SPELL AND ARITH- METIC DURING 3-YEARS AT THOS. S. BONNEAU'S SCHOOL IN HIS BOY- HOOD. IT WAS ILLEGAL TO TEACH SLAVES AND SOMETIMES FOR- BIDDEN BY LAW FOR FREE BLACKS. PAYNE TAUGHT HIMSELF SUCH SUBJECTS AS BOTANY, ZOOLOGY, GEOGRAPHY, LITERATURE, SCIENCE AND SEVERAL LANGUAGES. HE OPENED HIS FIRST SCHOOL IN 1829 BUT EXPENSES FORCED HIM

Geo
LEE

TO CLOSE. IN 1830, RE-OPENED WITH SOME SUCCESS. WHEN WILBERFORCE U., WAS ORGANIZED IN OHIO (1856) BY THE M.E. CHURCH, BISHOP PAYNE WAS ON THE BOARD. ON MAR 10,1863 HE PURCHASED THE SCHOOL PROPERTY FOR THE A.M.E CHURCH AND BECAME THE FIRST BLACK COLLEGE PRESIDENT IN AMERICA!

SOME SCHOOLS OPERATED ILLEGALLY. BLACKS CRUSADED FOR EDUCATION DESPITE STRONG OPPOSITION. MANY RELIGIOUS GROUPS FOUNDED SCHOOLS AND COLLEGES.

1979 GEO L. LEE FEATURE SERVICE

FIRST BLACK MAJOR IN THE UNION ARMY

MARTIN R. DELANY

MILITANT SPOKESMAN FOR BLACK FREEDOM WAS BORN FREE IN CHARLESTON, VA. NOT ALLOWED PUBLIC SCHOOLING HE LEARNED THRU A PRIMER AND SPELLING BOOK SECURED FROM A PEDDLER. THE FAMILY MOVED TO WESTERN PENNSYLVANIA WHERE THE CHILDREN WENT TO SCHOOL. IN 1831 HE WENT TO PITTSBURGH AND BECAME INVOLVED IN THE ANTI-SLAVERY AND AFRICAN SOCIETIES. HE DECIDED ON MEDICINE AND STUDIED UNDER A DR. MCDOWELL AND MASTERED THE KNOWLEDGE AND IN 1837 WAS QUALIFIED TO PRACTICE. IN 1849 HE GAINED ADMISSION TO HARVARD MEDICAL SCHOOL. BUT PREJUDICE FORCED HIM OUT. IN 1859 HE HEADED

1812
1885

GEO LEE

SPEAKING OF DELANY... PRESIDENT LINCOLN SAID: "THIS MOST EXTRAORDINARY AND INTELLIGENT BLACK MAN."

A SOLDIER
EXPLORER
AUTHOR
ABOLITIONIST
DOCTOR

A FIERY SPOKESMAN ON BLACK MANHOOD

© 1977 George L. Lee Feature Service

AN EXPLORATION TO AFRICA'S NIGER VALLEY FOR A "BACK-TO-AFRICA" MOVEMENT AND MADE A REPORT. DURING THE CIVIL WAR HE ASKED PRES. LINCOLN FOR AN ALL-BLACK UNIT WITH BLACK OFFICERS. HE WAS COMMISSIONED A FIELD MAJOR AND SENT TO CHARLESTON, S.C., TO COMMAND THE 104th U.S. NEGRO TROOPS.

ACCORDING TO HISTORIANS

MARY ELLEN PLEASANT

BETTER KNOWN AS "MAMMY PLEASANT", CIVIL RIGHTS ACTIVIST, HOUSEKEEPER, BOARDING HOUSE PROPRIETOR AND KNOWN THROUGHOUT SAN FRANCISCO IN THE MID-1800's FOR HER FINE SOUTHERN COOKING SHE SERVED SOME OF THE MOST INFLUENTIAL MEN OF THE 19th CENTURY IN HER BOARDING HOUSES. BORN A SLAVE ON AN AUGUSTA, GA., PLANTATION IN 1814. FREED BY HER MASTER AND GIVEN PASSAGE TO BOSTON. SHE MARRIED A WELL-TO-DO CUBAN WHOSE HOME WAS A MEETING PLACE FOR ABOLITIONISTS. HE DIED AND LEFT HER QUITE COMFORTABLE. THE CALIFORNIA GOLD RUSH WAS ON AND SHE WENT TO SAN FRANCISCO. BECAME A HOUSEKEEPER FOR THE WEALTHY. A GOOD BUSINESS WOMAN, SHE MADE MONEY IN THE STOCK MARKET. AIDED THE FREEDOM OF SLAVES AS AN AGENT OF THE UNDERGROUND RAILROAD. A FRIEND OF JOHN BROWN THE ABOLITIONIST, SHE OFFERED HIM $30,000 FOR THE MOVEMENT (1858). "MAMMY" WAS REFERRED TO AS THE "MOTHER OF CIVIL RIGHTS." HER LAWSUIT AGAINST THE SAN FRANCISCO STREET CAR CO., GAVE BLACKS... THE RIGHT TO RIDE. SHE FOUGHT AND WON... BLACKS THE RIGHT TO TESTIFY IN THE COURTS. SHE BECAME THE MOST INFLUENTIAL..... BLACK VOICE IN CITY... AND BENEFACTOR TO THE POOR! "MAMMY" DIED IN 1904 AT AGE OF 90. HER "LIFE" A MYSTERY TO HISTORIANS!

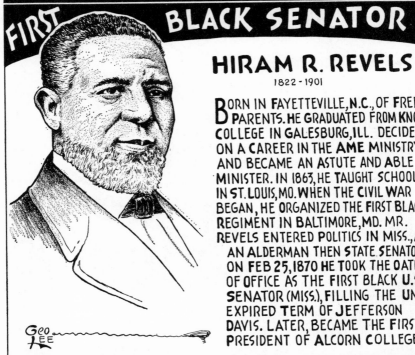

FIRST BLACK SENATOR

HIRAM R. REVELS
1822-1901

BORN IN FAYETTEVILLE, N.C., OF FREE PARENTS. HE GRADUATED FROM KNOX COLLEGE IN GALESBURG, ILL. DECIDED ON A CAREER IN THE AME MINISTRY AND BECAME AN ASTUTE AND ABLE MINISTER. IN 1863, HE TAUGHT SCHOOL IN ST. LOUIS, MO. WHEN THE CIVIL WAR BEGAN, HE ORGANIZED THE FIRST BLACK REGIMENT IN BALTIMORE, MD. MR. REVELS ENTERED POLITICS IN MISS., AS AN ALDERMAN THEN STATE SENATOR. ON FEB 25, 1870 HE TOOK THE OATH OF OFFICE AS THE FIRST BLACK U.S. SENATOR (MISS.), FILLING THE UNEXPIRED TERM OF JEFFERSON DAVIS. LATER, BECAME THE FIRST PRESIDENT OF ALCORN COLLEGE.

Geo Lee

DR. MORDECAI JOHNSON

A NATIVE OF COLUMBUS, TENN., WAS THE FIRST BLACK PRESIDENT OF HOWARD UNIVERSITY IN 1926 AT THE AGE OF 36. HE SERVED FOR 30-YEARS. THE SON OF A MINISTER, HE ALSO STUDIED FOR THE MINISTRY. HE PASTORED A BAPTIST CHURCH IN CHARLESTON, W.VA. EDUCATED AT MOREHOUSE, HARVARD AND GAMMON SEMINARY. WON SPINGARN MEDAL. (1929)

FIRST

6

BISHOP JAMES W. HEALY
1830 - 1900

FIRST NEGRO ROMAN CATHOLIC BISHOP IN AMERICA IN 1875. BORN NEAR MACON, GA., SON OF A SLAVE MOTHER AND IRISH PLANTER. AT 6 HE WAS SENT TO BOSTON TO BE EDUCATED. THE FIRST NEGRO STUDENT AT HOLY CROSS COLLEGE. STUDIED IN PARIS AND WAS ORDAINED A PRIEST IN NOTRE DAME CATHEDRAL IN 1854. SERVED AS FIRST CHANCELLOR OF THE DIOCESE IN BOSTON. ROSE TO BISHOP OF MAINE AND NEW HAMPSHIRE.

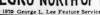

CONG. OSCAR DE PRIEST
1871 - 1951

A NATIVE OF ALABAMA, HE WENT TO CHICAGO, ILL., AS A YOUNG MAN. STARTED HIS CAREER AS A PLASTERER. ENTERED POLITICS AND REAL ESTATE. HE HELD CITY AND STATE OFFICES. IN 1928 HE WAS ELECTED TO THE U.S. CONGRESS, THE FIRST NEGRO NORTH OF THE OHIO RIVER.

7

A SOLDIER OF THE BLUE

HENRY MACK

BORN A SLAVE ON INDEPENDENCE DAY, 1836, IN FAYETTE CITY, ALA. HE STAYED WITH HIS MOTHER ON A PLANTATION UNTIL HE WAS 26 YEARS OLD. AFTER TROUBLE WITH THE OVERSEER IN THE PROTECTION OF HIS MOTHER, HE DECIDED TO SEEK FREEDOM. THEY ESCAPED TO A UNION ARMY CAMP AND ENLISTED, DEC 15, 1863 IN COMPANY "H", 57th REGIMENT, U.S. INFANTRY. HE WAS SENT SOUTH AND NEVER SAW HIS MOTHER AGAIN, ALTHO HE SEARCHED MANY YEARS AFTER THE WAR. HE SETTLED IN NEBRASKA AND MARRIED. HIS WIFE DIED AND HE MOVED TO MINNESOTA AND REMARRIED. MACK ALSO FOUGHT IN THE MEXICAN WAR. HE JOINED THE GEORGE N. MORGAN POST No.4, GRAND ARMY OF THE REPUBLIC. IN 1943 HIS COMRADES ELECTED HIM JUNIOR VICE-COMMANDER OF THE MINNESOTA G.A.R. LIVING IN MINNEAPOLIS IN DEC., 1944 HE BROKE HIS LEG. HE WAS 108 YEARS OLD. HENRY MACK DIED ON APRIL 4, 1945. REPORTEDLY THE OLDEST LIVING CIVIL WAR VETERAN AND WAS ACCORDED A FULL MILITARY FUNERAL!

DR. HENRY FITZBUTLER
1837 - 1901

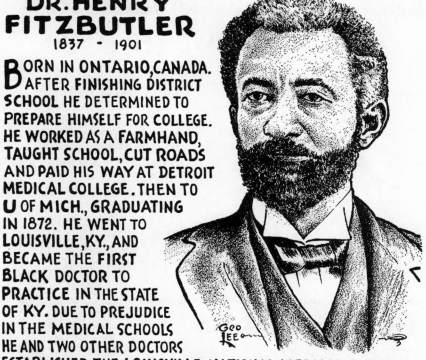

BORN IN ONTARIO, CANADA. AFTER FINISHING DISTRICT SCHOOL HE DETERMINED TO PREPARE HIMSELF FOR COLLEGE. HE WORKED AS A FARMHAND, TAUGHT SCHOOL, CUT ROADS AND PAID HIS WAY AT DETROIT MEDICAL COLLEGE. THEN TO U OF MICH., GRADUATING IN 1872. HE WENT TO LOUISVILLE, KY., AND BECAME THE FIRST BLACK DOCTOR TO PRACTICE IN THE STATE OF KY. DUE TO PREJUDICE IN THE MEDICAL SCHOOLS HE AND TWO OTHER DOCTORS ESTABLISHED THE LOUISVILLE NATIONAL MEDICAL COLLEGE IN 1888. HE WAS DEAN AND INSTRUCTOR IN MATERIA MEDICA AND SURGERY. TO AID HIS STUDENTS HE STARTED A HOSPITAL IN 1895.

HARRY T. BURLEIGH
1866 1949

COMPOSER, ARRANGER AND BARITONE SOLOIST. IN 1894 AT THE AGE OF 28 HE BECAME THE SOLOIST AT ST. GEORGE'S EPISCOPAL CHURCH IN N.Y.C. AT 82 HE WAS STILL SOLOIST. HE COMPOSED-"DEEP RIVER."

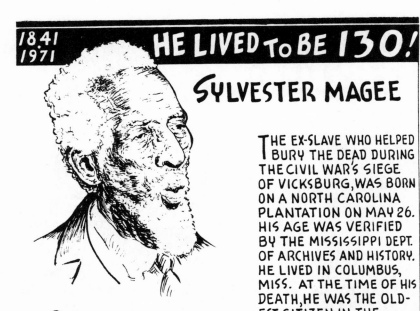

18.41
1971

HE LIVED TO BE 130!

SYLVESTER MAGEE

THE EX-SLAVE WHO HELPED BURY THE DEAD DURING THE CIVIL WAR'S SIEGE OF VICKSBURG, WAS BORN ON A NORTH CAROLINA PLANTATION ON MAY 26. HIS AGE WAS VERIFIED BY THE MISSISSIPPI DEPT. OF ARCHIVES AND HISTORY. HE LIVED IN COLUMBUS, MISS. AT THE TIME OF HIS DEATH, HE WAS THE OLDEST CITIZEN IN THE NATION!

Geo LEE

ROBERT SMALLS

1839
.
1915

THE EX-SLAVE WHO ROSE TO BE A CONGRESSMAN FROM SOUTH CAROLINA...WAS ONCE A PILOT ON THE STEAMER "THE PLANTER" IN 1862. HE STOLE THE BOAT AND RAN IT INTO THE UNION LINES; IT HAD VALUABLE WAR DISPATCHES AND CARGO. THE NAVY MADE HIM THE CHIEF PILOT. LATER HE WAS PROMOTED TO CAPTAIN.

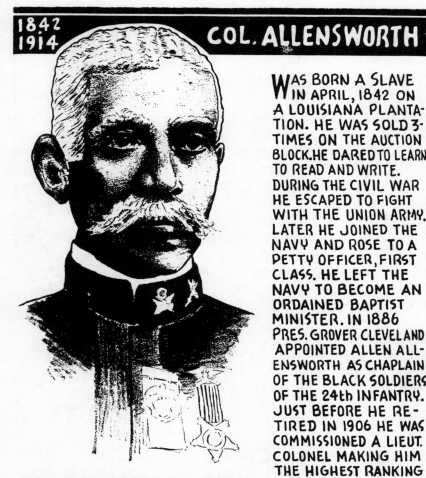

1842 1914

COL. ALLENSWORTH

WAS BORN A SLAVE IN APRIL, 1842 ON A LOUISIANA PLANTATION. HE WAS SOLD 3-TIMES ON THE AUCTION BLOCK. HE DARED TO LEARN TO READ AND WRITE. DURING THE CIVIL WAR HE ESCAPED TO FIGHT WITH THE UNION ARMY. LATER HE JOINED THE NAVY AND ROSE TO A PETTY OFFICER, FIRST CLASS. HE LEFT THE NAVY TO BECOME AN ORDAINED BAPTIST MINISTER. IN 1886 PRES. GROVER CLEVELAND APPOINTED ALLEN ALLENSWORTH AS CHAPLAIN OF THE BLACK SOLDIERS OF THE 24th INFANTRY. JUST BEFORE HE RETIRED IN 1906 HE WAS COMMISSIONED A LIEUT. COLONEL MAKING HIM THE HIGHEST RANKING BLACK OFFICER IN THE ARMY AT THE TIME.

ON AUG 3, 1908, ALLENSWORTH AS PRESIDENT OF THE CALIFORNIA COLONY AND HOME PROMOTION ASSOC., FOUNDED THE ALL-BLACK TOWN OF -ALLENSWORTH, CALIF.- IN THE SAN JOAQUIN VALLEY...70-MILES SOUTH OF FRESNO.

Geo Lee

T. McCANTS STEWART
1852 – 1923

DISTINGUISHED LAWYER, AUTHOR AND SCHOLAR WAS BORN IN CHARLESTON, S.C. HE GRADUATED FROM UNIV. OF S. CAR., WITH HONORS IN THE COLLEGE AND LAW DEPTS., IN 1875. BECAME A PROF. OF LETTERS AND LAW AT THE COLLEGE OF LIBERIA, W. AFRICA. IN 1886 HE WAS ADMITTED TO THE N.Y. STATE BAR. THE FIRST BLACK TO SERVE ON THE BROOKLYN BOARD OF EDUCATION (1891-95). A SUPERB ORATOR.

GEO LEE

JOSH WHITE
1908 – 1969

FAMOUS FOLK, BLUES AND SPIRITUAL SINGER WAS BORN IN GREENVILLE, S. CARO. IN 1943 HE TURNED DOWN $87,000 IN MOVIE OFFERS BECAUSE HE REFUSED TO TAKE ROLES THAT HE FELT WOULD DEGRADE NEGROES.

© 1970. George L. Lee Feature Service

12

FROM BRICKMAKER TO HOTEL-OWNER

A STORY OF A PIONEER WHO CONQUERED RACE PREJUDICE BY ACHIEVING A BUSINESS SUCCESS.

EDWARD C. BERRY
OF ATHENS, OHIO

1. BORN IN OBERLIN, OHIO IN 1854. WHEN HE WAS 2 HIS FAMILY MOVED TO ALBANY, O. HE WENT TO THE ALBANY PUBLIC SCHOOLS. AT 16 HIS FATHER DIED. THE ELDEST OF 9 CHILDREN HE HAD TO LOOK FOR WORK. HE WALKED 10 MI. TO ATHENS.

2. HE FOUND WORK IN A BRICK-YARD AT 50 CENTS-A-DAY. SOON HE WAS EARNING $1.25. BEING VERY ENTERPRISING HE WOULD SELL REFRESH-MENTS AT THE CIRCUS OR ON A TRAIN EXCURSION.

3. LATER WORKING IN A RESTAURANT HE BECAME PROFICIENT IN CATERING. WITH CAPITAL OF $40 HE OPENED A LUNCH COUNTER. IN 1878 WITH HIS WIFE HE OPENED A RESTAURANT; IT WAS A SUCCESS. SALESMEN WHO DINED THERE URGED

4. HIM TO BUILD A HOTEL. IN 1893 HE DECIDED TO ENTER THE HOTEL FIELD AND BUILT THE HOTEL BERRY. WITH RACIAL TENSION AGAINST HIM AND THE PANIC OF 1893, MADE THINGS VERY DIFFICULT. BUT A LOAN FROM A FRIEND AND GOOD SERVICE HE HELD ON. BUSINESS PROSPERED AND HE BECAME ATHENS' LEADING HOTEL-KEEPER.

Geo Lee

© 1977 George L. Lee Feature Service

LUCY CRAFT LANEY
1854 – 1933

BORN IN SLAVERY IN GEORGIA. SHE WAS TAUGHT TO READ AND WRITE BY HER MASTER'S SISTER. AFTER FREEDOM SHE SOUGHT AN EDUCATION AT ATLANTA U., AND WAS ONE OF THE FIRST FOUR GRADUATES IN 1873. A TEACHER, SHE WAS EAGER TO EDUCATE HER PEOPLE. SHE STARTED A SCHOOL IN THE BASEMENT OF A CHURCH. IT GREW INTO THE HAINES NORMAL INDUSTRIAL INSTITUTE.

ALEXANDRE DUMAS
1802 – 1870

FAMOUS AUTHOR AND PLAYWRIGHT OF THE 19TH CENTURY WROTE 1200 VOLUMES DURING HIS CAREER. HE ONCE TURNED OUT 60 FULL-LENGTH NOVELS IN A SINGLE YEAR. IN 1844 HE PRODUCED TWO OF THE MOST POPULAR NOVELS EVER WRITTEN: "THE 3 MUSKETEERS" AND "THE COUNT OF MONTE CRISTO."

DR. NATHAN F. MOSSELL

THE FIRST BLACK GRADUATE OF THE UNIV. OF PENNSYLVANIA, FROM ITS MEDICAL SCHOOL. HE WAS BORN IN HAMILTON, ONTARIO, CANADA IN JULY, 1856. HE ENTERED LINCOLN UNIV., IN 1874 AND GRADUATED WITH HONORS IN 1879. THAT FALL HE ENROLLED IN THE MEDICAL DEPT., OF THE U. OF PENN., THE FIRST OF HIS RACE. HE WAS THE FIRST BLACK TO BE ADMITTED TO THE PHILA., COUNTY MEDICAL SOCIETY (1888). IN 1895 HE FOUNDED THE FREDERICK DOUGLASS MEMORIAL HOSPITAL AND TRAINING SCHOOL IN PHILADELPHIA TO TRAIN BLACK GIRLS AS NURSES.

Geo. Lee

PEARL PRIMUS

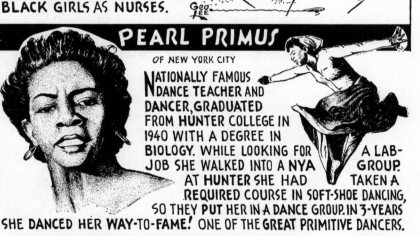

OF NEW YORK CITY

NATIONALLY FAMOUS DANCE TEACHER AND DANCER, GRADUATED FROM HUNTER COLLEGE IN 1940 WITH A DEGREE IN BIOLOGY. WHILE LOOKING FOR A LAB-JOB SHE WALKED INTO A NYA GROUP. AT HUNTER SHE HAD TAKEN A REQUIRED COURSE IN SOFT-SHOE DANCING, SO THEY PUT HER IN A DANCE GROUP. IN 3-YEARS SHE DANCED HER WAY-TO-FAME! ONE OF THE GREAT PRIMITIVE DANCERS.

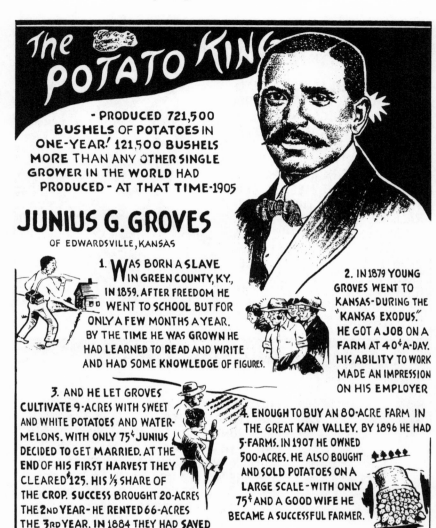

The POTATO KING

- PRODUCED 721,500 BUSHELS OF POTATOES IN ONE-YEAR! 121,500 BUSHELS MORE THAN ANY OTHER SINGLE GROWER IN THE WORLD HAD PRODUCED - AT THAT TIME-1905

JUNIUS G. GROVES

OF EDWARDSVILLE, KANSAS

1. WAS BORN A SLAVE IN GREEN COUNTY, KY., IN 1859. AFTER FREEDOM HE WENT TO SCHOOL BUT FOR ONLY A FEW MONTHS A YEAR. BY THE TIME HE WAS GROWN HE HAD LEARNED TO READ AND WRITE AND HAD SOME KNOWLEDGE OF FIGURES.

2. IN 1879 YOUNG GROVES WENT TO KANSAS-DURING THE "KANSAS EXODUS." HE GOT A JOB ON A FARM AT 40¢ A-DAY. HIS ABILITY TO WORK MADE AN IMPRESSION ON HIS EMPLOYER

3. AND HE LET GROVES CULTIVATE 9-ACRES WITH SWEET AND WHITE POTATOES AND WATER-MELONS. WITH ONLY 75¢ JUNIUS DECIDED TO GET MARRIED. AT THE END OF HIS FIRST HARVEST THEY CLEARED $125. HIS ⅓ SHARE OF THE CROP. SUCCESS BROUGHT 20-ACRES THE 2ND YEAR- HE RENTED 66-ACRES THE 3RD YEAR. IN 1884 THEY HAD SAVED

4. ENOUGH TO BUY AN 80-ACRE FARM IN THE GREAT KAW VALLEY. BY 1896 HE HAD 5-FARMS. IN 1907 HE OWNED 500-ACRES. HE ALSO BOUGHT AND SOLD POTATOES ON A LARGE SCALE - WITH ONLY 75¢ AND A GOOD WIFE HE BECAME A SUCCESSFUL FARMER.

Geo LEE

BUSINESSMAN

J. L. THOMAS

BORN A SLAVE ON A PLANTATION NEAR TROY, ALABAMA. AFTER FREEDOM HIS MOTHER AND FAMILY MOVED TO PINE LEVEL. THEN TO UNION SPRINGS, WHERE SHE FOUND WORK AS A COOK FOR $2.00 A-MONTH AND THE USE OF A ONE ROOM HOUSE. YOUNG THOMAS WAS HIRED OUT AT 50 CENTS A-MONTH. AFTER A YEAR HE EARNED $2.00 A-MONTH. LATER HIS MOTHER HIRED HIM OUT TO A BLACK FARMER NAMED THOMPSON FOR $5 A-MONTH. FOR THE FIRST TIME HE REALIZED THAT SOME BLACK MEN WERE INDEPENDENT AND IT MARKED AN EPOCH IN HIS LIFE. HE WORKED HARD AND SAVED HIS MONEY. HE LEFT THE FARM AND HIRED OUT TO RUN A PUBLIC DRAY FOR $10. SOON

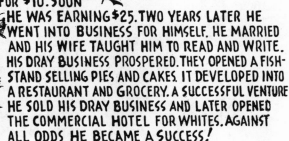

HE WAS EARNING $25. TWO YEARS LATER HE WENT INTO BUSINESS FOR HIMSELF. HE MARRIED AND HIS WIFE TAUGHT HIM TO READ AND WRITE. HIS DRAY BUSINESS PROSPERED. THEY OPENED A FISH-STAND SELLING PIES AND CAKES. IT DEVELOPED INTO A RESTAURANT AND GROCERY. A SUCCESSFUL VENTURE HE SOLD HIS DRAY BUSINESS AND LATER OPENED THE COMMERCIAL HOTEL FOR WHITES. AGAINST ALL ODDS HE BECAME A SUCCESS!

FAMOUS EDUCATOR

1863
1939

DEAN KELLY MILLER

DEAN EMERITUS OF HOWARD UNIVERSITY'S LIBERAL ARTS COLLEGE AT THE TIME OF HIS DEATH. BORN AT WINNSBORO, S.C. AS A BOY, HIS SKILL IN MATHEMATICS ATTRACTED ATTENTION AND HE WAS BROUGHT TO WASH., D.C. TO ENTER HOWARD U. HE GRADUATED IN 1886. HE PURSUED POSTGRADUATE STUDIES AT JOHNS HOPKINS AND, AFTERWARDS, SPENT A YEAR TEACHING IN HIGH SCHOOLS IN WASHINGTON. HE THEN WENT TO HOWARD TO TEACH AND REMAINED THERE

FOR 40-YEARS. ONE OF THE FIRST BLACK SCHOLARS, HE SPENT MANY YEARS IN THE STRUGGLE FOR EDUCATIONAL AND CULTURAL IMPROVEMENTS OF HIS PEOPLE. A BRILLIANT SPEAKER HE WAS ALSO A PROLIFIC WRITER OF BOOKS AND NEWSPAPER ARTICLES.

© 1976, George L. Lee Feature Service

FROM PEDDLER TO BANKER

ANTHONY OVERTON

1865
1946

BORN IN MONROE, LA., HE WAS EDUCATED AT WASHBURN COLLEGE EARNING A SCIENCE DEGREE. LATER A LAW DEGREE FROM U. OF KANSAS IN 1888 AND ADMITTED TO THE BAR THE SAME YEAR. SERVED AS JUDGE IN SHAWNEE CTY, KANS, FOR 2-YEARS. MARRIED AND WENT TO WANAMAKER, INDIAN TERR., WHERE HE OPENED A GENERAL STORE. HE PROSPERED — BUT WAS ROBBED BY THE DALTON GANG. HE MOVED TO KANSAS CITY WHERE HE FIRST STARTED MANUFACTURING BAKING

WINNER OF THE (NAACP) SPINGARN MEDAL IN 1937.

Geo. LEE

HARMON FOUNDATION AWARD IN 1928

POWDER, EXTRACTS AND STARCH... LATER TOILET ARTICLES. HE PEDDLED HIS PRODUCTS ALL OVER THE SOUTH. THIS LED TO THE OVERTON HYGIENICS CO., WHICH HE LOCATED IN CHICAGO IN 1911 AND DEVELOPED INTO THE COSMETICS BUSINESS. IN 1922 STARTED THE DOUGLASS NATIONAL BANK... THEN THE VICTORY MUTUAL INS. CO. THEY BOTH THRIVED UNTIL THE DEPRESSION (1932). HE ALSO PUBLISHED THE "CHICAGO BEE" PAPER.

PORTER TO BANKER

$

JESSE BINGA
1865 - 1950

A SELF-MADE BANKER WAS BORN IN DETROIT, MICH. WITH ONLY A HIGH SCHOOL EDUCATION AND A LITTLE EXPERIENCE IN REAL ESTATE, HE HAD GAINED THRU MANAGING SOME OLD TENEMENT BUILDINGS OWNED BY HIS MOTHER IN DETROIT, HE WENT TO CHICAGO IN 1893. HIS FIRST JOB...A PULLMAN PORTER. BUT A DESIRE TO WORK FOR HIM-SELF...HE BECAME A HUCKSTER... ON CHICAGO'S SOUTHSIDE AS FAR AS 35th ST. HE MET AND MARRIED EUDORA JOHNSON. A DAUGHTER OF "MUSHMOUTH JOHNSON" A WELL-TO -DO GAMBLER. MRS. BINGA INHERIT-ED HER FATHER'S MONEY WHEN HE DIED. MR. BINGA OPENED A REAL

ESTATE OFFICE AT 36th PL & STATE. HE THRIVED...OPENED A PRIVATE BANK...HE CONTINUED TO ACQUIRE PROPERTY. HE OBTAINED A STATE CHARTER FOR HIS BANK AND MOVED TO 35th & STATE, BUYING THE CORNER HE ERECTED THE BINGA ARCADE BUILDING FOR ... A HALF-A-MILLION! IN 1929 THE DEPRESSION HIT...ALONG WITH OTH-ER BANKS...BINGA CLOSED-JULY 1930.

GEO LEE

© 1974 George L. Lee Feature Service

JUMP, SIM! JUMP!

1874 · 1957

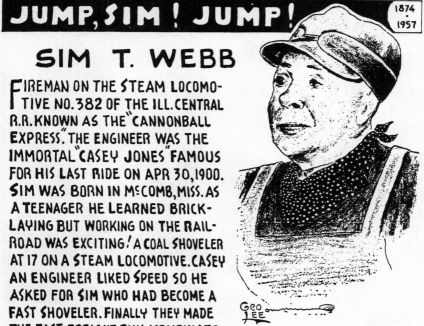

SIM T. WEBB

FIREMAN ON THE STEAM LOCOMO-TIVE NO. 382 OF THE ILL. CENTRAL R.R. KNOWN AS THE "CANNONBALL EXPRESS". THE ENGINEER WAS THE IMMORTAL "CASEY JONES" FAMOUS FOR HIS LAST RIDE ON APR 30, 1900. SIM WAS BORN IN McCOMB, MISS. AS A TEENAGER HE LEARNED BRICK-LAYING BUT WORKING ON THE RAIL-ROAD WAS EXCITING! A COAL SHOVELER AT 17 ON A STEAM LOCOMOTIVE. CASEY AN ENGINEER LIKED SPEED SO HE ASKED FOR SIM WHO HAD BECOME A FAST SHOVELER. FINALLY THEY MADE THE FAST FREIGHT RUN MEMPHIS TO

Geo LEE

JUMP, SIM! JUMP!

AFTER HIS BRO-KEN LEG HEAL-ED, HE STAYED ON FOR 18 YRS THEN TO BRICK-LAYING. HE LIVED TO BE 83 BUT NEVER FORGOT CASEY'S FAMOUS LAST WORDS-"JUMP, SIM! JUMP!"

1984 Geo L. Lee Feature Service

CANTON, MISS. ON APR 29, 1900... THEY WERE ASKED TO DOUBLE TO CANTON. THEY TOOK No. 382. A LATE START BUT 90 MPH SOON MADE UP THE TIME. NEAR VAUGHAN, MISS A FREIGHT WAS MAKING IT OFF BUT STALLED ON THE MAIN LINE. CASEY TRIED TO STOP... IT WAS TOO LATE. HE TOLD SIM TO JUMP. THE CANN-ONBALL EXPRESS" CRASHED, KILLED CASEY. A SONG IMMORTALIZED HIM!

DR. MARY MᶜLEOD BETHUNE
1875 - 1955

WHO WAS AWARDED THE THOMAS JEFFERSON MEDAL FOR BEING NAMED THE "OUTSTANDING WOMAN OF THE YEAR" IN 1942 – ONCE WALKED BAREFOOT ACROSS PLOWED FIELDS TO GET HER FIRST BOOK "LEARNING" IN THE RURAL SCHOOL FOR NEGRO CHILDREN NEAR MAYSVILLE, S.C. LATER WITH DETERMINATION AND A SOAP-BOX FOR A DESK SHE FOUNDED THE NOW FAMOUS BETHUNE-COOKMAN COLLEGE IN DAYTONA BEACH, FLA.

HE MADE THE FIRST CLOCK IN U.S.
BENJAMIN BANNEKER
1731 - 1806

BORN FREE IN MARYLAND. IN 1761 HE CARVED A CLOCK FROM WOOD THAT RAN FOR 20-YEARS. IN ASTRONOMY AND MATHEMATICS HE EXCELLED. FOR 10-YEARS HE PUBLISHED AN ALMANAC FOR FARMERS. IN 1791 HE HELPED SURVEY THE NEW FEDERAL CITY OF WASHINGTON D.C.

Geo
LEE

22

HIS HONOR THE JUDGE..

JUDGE ARMOND W. SCOTT

1875
1960

Known as the Humanitarian in the administration of justice...His sympathetic and scientific approach of the problems of law violators in the Municipal Court in Wash, D.C. Appointed to the judgeship by Pres. Roosevelt in 1935. Born in Wilmington, N.C. He received his A.B. at Biddle U. (now Johnson C. Smith U.) at Charlotte, N.C. and his Law Degree (LL.B) from Shaw U. Scott started his practice in Wilmington but his outspoken views on Jim

Geo Lee

"I'M AS SOBER AS A JUDGE... YER HONOR"

"GUILTY!"

-30- DAYS!

JUDGE SCOTT SENTENCED THOUSANDS TO JAIL, DRUNKS, PROSTITUTES AND THIEVES IF THEY WERE GUILTY. HE DID HIS BEST TO ESTABLISH CLINKS TO HELP THE WAYWARD.

Crow forced him to leave. He went to Wash, D.C. and continued. In 1904 he was admitted to the bar of the U.S. Supreme Court. Scott was the first Black judge in the New Deal administration and served for 22 years. He received the Laurel Wreath, the highest award of the Kappa Alpha Psi Frat., for outstanding service!

1979 GEO L. LEE FEATURE SERVICE

23

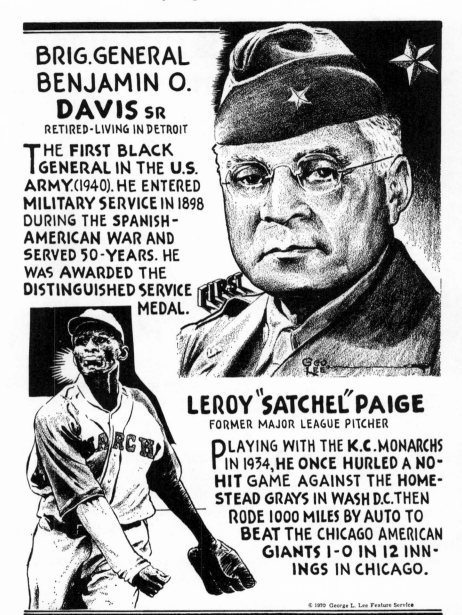

BRIG. GENERAL BENJAMIN O. DAVIS SR
RETIRED - LIVING IN DETROIT

THE **FIRST BLACK GENERAL** IN THE **U.S. ARMY.** (1940). HE ENTERED **MILITARY SERVICE** IN 1898 DURING THE **SPANISH-AMERICAN** WAR AND SERVED 50-YEARS. HE WAS AWARDED THE **DISTINGUISHED SERVICE** MEDAL.

LEROY "SATCHEL" PAIGE
FORMER MAJOR LEAGUE PITCHER

PLAYING WITH THE **K.C. MONARCHS** IN 1934, HE ONCE HURLED A NO-HIT GAME AGAINST THE HOME-STEAD GRAYS IN WASH D.C. THEN RODE 1000 MILES BY AUTO TO BEAT THE CHICAGO AMERICAN GIANTS 1-0 IN 12 INN-INGS IN CHICAGO.

PUBLISHER

ROBERT L. VANN

WHO ROSE FROM THE OBSCURITY OF A BACK-WOODS FARM "OUT FROM" AHOSKIE, N.C., TO BE WITH U.S. PRESIDENTS TO TALK ABOUT THE NEGRO. EDUCATED AT VIRGINIA UNION UNIV. AND THE U. OF PITTSBURGH. HE WAS ADMITTED TO THE BAR IN 1909 AND PRACTISED LAW IN PITTSBURGH. IN 1910 HE WAS ONE OF THE FOUNDERS OF THE PITTSBURGH COURIER, AND UNDER HIS LEADERSHIP IT BECAME AMERICA'S No. 1 BLACK NEWSPAPER. MR. VANN SERVED AS ASS'T CITY SOLICITOR AND AS SPECIAL ASS'T TO THE ATTORNEY GENERAL IN WASH., D.C. A COURAGEOUS, MILITANT LEADER WHO FOUGHT FOR THE RIGHTS OF HIS PEOPLE... AN EDITOR WHO BELIEVED IN HIS CONVICT-IONS. ONE OF AMERICA'S DISTINGUISHED SONS. DURING WORLD WAR II IN 1943 A U.S. LIBERTY SHIP WAS LAUNCHED IN HIS HONOR – "SS ROBERT L. VANN"... IT WAS HIT AND SUNK, MAR 1, 1945.

WILLIAM PICKENS

IN 1904, WHILE WORKING HIS WAY THROUGH YALE UNIVERSITY HE WON THE HIGHEST ORATORICAL PRIZE GIVEN BY THAT UNIVERSITY...THE TEN EYCK PRIZE. THE FIRST BLACK TO WIN THE COVETED HONOR. AN EDUCATOR, HE WAS DEAN OF MORGAN COLLEGE FROM 1915-1920. SECRETARY AND DIRECTOR OF BRANCHES FOR THE NAACP (1920-42). DIRECTOR OF THE INTERRACIAL SECTION OF THE U.S.TREASURY DEFENSE SAVINGS UNTIL 1952. AUTHOR OF MANY BOOKS INCLUDING "THE NEW NEGRO." DIED 1954 AT 73.

Geo LEE

JOHN ROY LYNCH

BORN OF A SLAVE MOTHER AND A WHITE PLANTER FATHER NEAR CONCORDIA PARISH, LA., IN 1847. HE WENT TO MISSISSIPPI WHERE HE BECAME A PHOTOGRAPHER AND LAWYER. HE ENTERED POLITICS AT 21 AND WAS ELECTED TO THE U.S. CONGRESS FROM MISS...THE FIRST BLACK AND THE YOUNGEST MEMBER (25-YRS) OF THE 43rd CONGRESS IN 1873. RE-ELECTED 1875 AND 1881. ALSO SPEAKER OF THE HOUSE.

26

DR. CHANNING TOBIAS
1882 - 1961

A NATIVE OF AUGUSTA, GA. EDUCATED AT PAINE COLLEGE. BECAME A C.M.E., ORDAINED MINISTER. RECEIVED HIS B.D. AT DREW THEOLOGICAL SEMINARY IN N.J. IN 1905. PROF. OF BIBLE LITERATURE AT PAINE FOR 6 YEARS. JOINED THE YMCA STAFF AND RETIRED AFTER 35 YEARS, AS SENIOR SEC'Y OF THE NAT'L COUNCIL. DIRECTOR OF THE PHELPS-STOKES FUND. THE FIRST NEGRO CHAIRMAN OF THE BOARD OF TRUSTEES OF HAMPTON INSTITUTE IN 1946. A CHAIRMAN OF THE NAACP BOARD, ALWAYS FOUGHT FOR FREEDOM.

Geo LEE

AIN'T MISBEHAVIN'

THOMAS 'FATS' WALLER
1904 - 1943

HONEYSUCKLE ROSE

F IRST MUSICIAN TO PLAY JAZZ ON THE PIPE ORGAN AND THE HAMMOND ORGAN. BORN IN N.Y.C., HE QUIT SCHOOL AT 15 TO TAKE A JOB PLAYING THE ORGAN IN A THEATRE. HE WAS FIRED WHEN HE PLAYED THE BLUES DURING A DEATH SCENE.

LIFE BEGINS AT 40

1882-1956

ROBERT A. COLE

SEVENTH **S**ON OF AN EX-SLAVE COTTON FARMER WHO INVESTED $500.00 IN A FAILING BURIAL ASSN., TO BECOME THE PRESIDENT OF THE CHICAGO METROPOLITAN ASSURANCE CO., WITH 74-MILLION IN FORCE (1953). BORN ON A SMALL FARM OWNED BY HIS PARENTS, NEAR MT. CARMEL, TENN. WITH LITTLE FORMAL EDUCATION – HE DID LEARN TO COUNT. AMBITIOUS HE WENT TO WORK IN THE I.C. RAIL YARDS IN PADUCAH, KY. IN 1905 HE DECIDED TO TRY HIS LUCK IN CHICAGO. AFTER BUS-BOY JOBS

NOW YOU CAN BE ASSURED OF A FINE BURIAL...FOR ONLY 20¢ A-WEEK.

R.A.COLE

Geo Lee

HE LOOKED FOR SOMETHING BETTER...BECAME A PULLMAN PORTER FOR 14-YEARS. MADE GOOD MONEY ...SPENT IT FASTER...BY THE AGE OF 40...HE WAS BROKE BUT VOWED TO SAVE. AND DID. WITH $500 IN 1927 HE INVESTED IN A SHAKY BURIAL ASSN. HE SOLD DEATH BENEFITS TO POOR PEOPLE AND PROSPERED. BY 1953 IT HAD GROWN TO OVER 7-MILLION IN ASSETS.'

© 1976 George L. Lee Feature Service

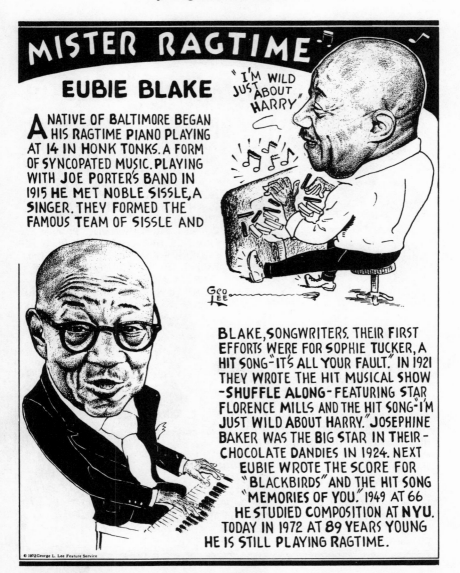

MISTER RAGTIME

EUBIE BLAKE

"I'M WILD JUST ABOUT HARRY"

A NATIVE OF BALTIMORE BEGAN HIS RAGTIME PIANO PLAYING AT 14 IN HONK TONKS. A FORM OF SYNCOPATED MUSIC. PLAYING WITH JOE PORTER'S BAND IN 1915 HE MET NOBLE SISSLE, A SINGER. THEY FORMED THE FAMOUS TEAM OF SISSLE AND

GEO LEE

BLAKE, SONGWRITERS. THEIR FIRST EFFORTS WERE FOR SOPHIE TUCKER, A HIT SONG-"IT'S ALL YOUR FAULT." IN 1921 THEY WROTE THE HIT MUSICAL SHOW -SHUFFLE ALONG- FEATURING STAR FLORENCE MILLS AND THE HIT SONG-"I'M JUST WILD ABOUT HARRY." JOSEPHINE BAKER WAS THE BIG STAR IN THEIR-CHOCOLATE DANDIES IN 1924. NEXT EUBIE WROTE THE SCORE FOR "BLACKBIRDS" AND THE HIT SONG "MEMORIES OF YOU." 1949 AT 66 HE STUDIED COMPOSITION AT NYU. TODAY IN 1972 AT 89 YEARS YOUNG HE IS STILL PLAYING RAGTIME.

© 1972 George L. Lee Feature Service

Eubie Blake died on February 12, 1983. He was 100 years and 5 days old.

NEW ORLEANS JAZZ

OSCAR 'PAPA' CELESTIN

BORN IN NAPOLEONVILLE, LA., IN 1884. HE WAS ONE OF SIX CHILDREN OF A SUGAR CANE CUTTER AND HIS WIFE. AT AN EARLY AGE HE SAW HIS FIRST SHOW BOAT. WATCHING THE CORNET PLAYER HE KNEW HE WANTED A HORN. ABOUT 1900, ON ONE OF THE PLANTATIONS WHERE HIS FATHER WORKED, HE WAS GIVEN A BATTERED CORNET. FROM THEN ON... PRACTICE... PRACTICE, UNTIL HE COULD PLAY FOR CHURCH SOCIALS... JUST FOR FUN. BY 1906 HE HAD TAUGHT HIMSELF TO PLAY A GOOD, HARD HORN. HE WENT TO NEW ORLEANS, AND GOT A JOB AS A LONGSHOREMAN BY DAY.

Geo Lee

AT NIGHT HE TOOK HIS HORN TO THE TENDERLOIN DISTRICTS. HE DISCOVERED NEW SOUNDS AND PLAYED HOT MUSIC AT PLACES LIKE JOSIE ARLINGTON'S AND THE COUNTESS'PLACE. HE MET KING OLIVER, AL PICOU, BUDDY BOLDEN AND BUNK JOHNSON. PAPA BELIEVED IN GOOD SOLID JAZZ. HE ORGANIZED THE TUXEDO BAND, A MARCHING BAND AND PROBABLY THE FIRST JAZZ BAND IN AMERICA. BY 1930 PAPA HAD BECOME A LEGEND. DURING WORLD WAR II HIS MUSIC CAME TO A STANDSTILL. IN 1947 HE MADE HIS COMEBACK AND SOON WAS ON TOP. HIS GREATEST MOMENT WAS IN MAY 1953 AT THE WHITE HOUSE WHEN PRESIDENT "IKE" CONGRATULATED HIM. PAPA DIED IN 1954.

MAN THAT'S PAPA!

LOUIS ARMSTRONG NICKNAMED OSCAR CELESTIN "PAPA."

PAPA WOULD PLAY FOR 20-HOURS TO PROVE HIS STAMINA...

© 1974 George L. Lee Feature Service

JOE 'KING' OLIVER

1885-
1938

ONE OF THE GREAT JAZZ CORNETISTS OF HIS DAY. HE DID MUCH TO PROMOTE JAZZ IN AMERICA. BORN IN NEW ORLEANS, LA., HE STARTED HIS CAREER PLAYING IN STORYVILLE A RED-LIGHT DISTRICT AT THE 25 CLUB. HE TAUGHT THE GREAT LOUIS ARMSTRONG. IN 1917 STORYVILLE WAS SHUT DOWN AND HE TOOK HIS JAZZ

Geo
LEE

UP NORTH TO CHICAGO AND HELPED TO MAKE THE ROYAL GARDENS FAMOUS...AFTER-HOURS HE PLAYED THE DREAMLAND CAFE. IN 1920 HE FORMED HIS OWN BAND AND MOVED TO THE DREAMLAND. AFTER A YEAR HE WENT TO CALIFORNIA. HE RETURNED TO CHICAGO IN 1922 AND SENT FOR ARMSTRONG TO JOIN KING OLIVER'S CREOLE JAZZ BAND; TOGETHER THEY MADE JAZZ HISTORY. THEIR RECORDINGS WERE BIG HITS..."SUGARFOOT STOMP","CANAL STREET BLUES," AND "SOMEDAY SWEETHEART." THE DEPRESSION ENDED HIS CAREER.

JAZZ - IMMORTAL

1886
1973

EDWARD 'KID' ORY

Legendary Dixieland Jazz great whose career lasted 75 years.

THE MOST FAMOUS EXPONENT OF THE "TAILGATE" TROMBONE.

Geo Lee

THE "KID" WAS BORN ON CHRISTMAS DAY IN LA PLACE, LA. HIS CAREER STARTED IN N'ORLEANS THE BIRTHPLACE OF JAZZ AT THE AGE OF 10. BY 15, HE FORMED HIS OWN BAND. PLAYED IN THE BAWDYHOUSES IN STORYVILLE, THE RED-LIGHT DISTRICT OF N'ORLEANS AT 21. GAVE JOE OLIVER AND LOUIS ARMSTRONG THEIR FIRST JOBS. THE JAZZ SCENE MOVED TO CHICAGO IN 1919. ORY FOLLOWED IN 1925 AND PLAYED WITH ARMSTRONG'S, "HOT FIVE". AMONG HIS COMPOSITIONS WERE "MUSKRAT RAMBLE", AND "SAVOY BLUES." DURING THE DEPRESSION HE WENT TO LOS ANGELES AND RAISED CHICKENS. IN THE 1940's HE MADE A COMEBACK. PLAYED IN THE MOVIE- NEW ORLEANS. (1947)

THE KID STARTED HIS TAILGATE STYLE, TO KEEP FROM HITTING THE OTHERS WITH HIS SLIDE TROMBONE

CHOIR DIRECTOR

IN 1951 THE HALL JOHNSON CHOIR TOURED EUROPE FOR THE U.S. STATE DEPT.

HALL JOHNSON
1888 - 1970

WHO WAS HONORED IN 1966 AS THE "WORLD'S GREATEST CHOIR DIRECTOR", WAS BORN IN ATHENS, GA. UNTIL HE WAS 20 HE STUDIED THE VIOLIN, TEACHING HIMSELF. LATER STUDIED AT THE HAHN SCHOOL OF MUSIC (PHILA) AND THE U. OF PENN. RECEIVED HIS DOCTORATE FROM THE PHILA., MUSIC ACADEMY (1934). HE GAVE UP THE VIOLIN IN 1925 TO FORM THE HALL JOHNSON CHOIR. HE PRESERVED THE NEGRO SPIRITUALS. STARTING WITH 8 VOICES, HE ROSE TO 30 FOR THE PULITZER PRIZE PLAY "GREEN PASTURES"... HE WROTE THE MUSIC. A TREMENDOUS DIRECTOR, HIS FAMOUS EASTER CANTATA "THE SON OF MAN" WAS PRESENTED IN THE N.Y. CITY CENTER IN 1946 WITH SOLOISTS AND A CHORUS OF 300! COMPOSER OF SPIRITUALS.

Geo Lee

A DISTINGUISHED ACTOR

CLARENCE MUSE

AN OUTSTANDING CHARACTER ACTOR AND HIGHLY TALENTED PERSONALITY. A RADIO STAR, DRAMATIC BARITONE, PRODUCER, WRITER AND COMPOSER. BORN IN BALTIMORE ON OCT 7, 1889. IN 1911 HE GRADUATED FROM DICKERSON U., WITH A LAW DEGREE...BUT SOUGHT THE STAGE INSTEAD. BECAME A CONCERT SINGER, PLAYED VAUDEVILLE AND SANG ON RADIO. HE DESIRED AN ACTING CAR-

EER AND HELPED TO ORGANIZE A STOCK COMPANY IN HARLEM ...THE LAFAYETTE PLAYERS. MR. MUSE LEARNED THE ART OF CHARACTER ROLES AND WAS ONE OF THE LEADING ACTORS OF HIS DAY. IN 1928 HE WAS OFFERED ONE OF THE LEADS IN "HEARTS IN DIXIE" THE SECOND ALL-TALKIE MOVIE. HE STAYED IN HOLLYWOOD AND APPEARED IN 218 FILMS. HIS LAST ONE IN 1976..."CAR WASH"...AT THE AGE OF 87! HE COMPOSED THE HIT SONG, "WHEN IT'S SLEEPY TIME DOWN SOUTH."

HIS TELEVISION CREDITS: KRAFT MUSIC HALL, PLAYHOUSE 90, HALLMARK HALL OF FAME. HIS ACHIEVEMENTS WERE MANY!

GEO LEE

1979 GEO L. LEE FEATURE SERVICE

LOOKING BACK TO THE FORTIES

SINCLAIR HENRY JETER

1944 IN SEPTEMBER 1944 JETER THE ONLY BLACK ARTIFICIAL LEG MAKER IN THE U.S. AND THE ONLY PERSON TO MAKE A LATERAL MOTION LIMB WHICH OPERATED AS A NATURAL LIMB...... SECURED HIS PATENT No. 2215525. THE FISHER BODY CO., SOUGHT HIS PATENT BUT HE REFUSED. A FRIEND LOST BOTH LEGS MANY YEARS AGO. BUT HE COULDN'T RAISE THE MONEY FOR ARTIFICIAL LIMBS SO JETER A CARPEN- TER DECIDED TO TRY AND HE SUCCEEDED ALTHO HE HAD NEVER SEEN ONE MADE. FOR 36-YEARS HE MADE LIMBS IN HIS OWN SHOP IN DOVER PLAINS, N.Y. (POP.800) IN 1944 LIMBS ARE MASS PRODUCED... BUT SINCLAIR JETER, MASTER OF HIS ART CONTINUES BY HAND!

GEO LEE

© 1971. George L. Lee Feature Service

♪ SONGWRITERS ♪

CHARLES 'LUCKY' ROBERTS

TOP COMPOSER, PIANIST AND CONDUCTOR LEARNED TO PLAY THE PIANO BY THE TIME HE WAS 5-YEARS OLD. A NATIVE OF PHILADELPHIA, HE WROTE THE BIG HIT SONG "MOONLIGHT COCKTAIL RENDEZVOUS" IN 1912. HOWEVER IT WAS NOT UNTIL 1943 WHEN GLENN MILLER'S BAND MADE IT FAMOUS. HE WROTE RAGTIME...A BROADWAY MUSICAL SCORE FOR "SHY AND SLY" (1915)..."MAGNOLIA"..."I WANT TO BE EXCLUSIVELY WITH YOU"..."WHISTLIN' PETE", AND MANY, MANY OTHERS.

BUDDY JOHNSON

WELL KNOWN BAND LEADER, COMPOSER WROTE "BABY DON'T YOU CRY"... "LET'S BEAT OUT SOME LOVE"... "I AIN'T MAD AT YOU". WHEN HE WAS 11 HE WROTE "LET'S STOP PRETENDING", YEARS LATER IT WAS RECORDED BY DECCA AND BECAME A BEST SELLER. (1941)

RICHARD M. JONES

NOTED COMPOSER AND PIANIST AND ONE OF NEW ORLEANS FIRST "JAZZ KINGS" WAS BORN IN KY. A MUSIC SCOUT FOR THE OKEH RECORD CO., IN THE 20'S, HE WAS THE FIRST TO RECORD THE VOICE OF CAB CALLOWAY AND LOUIS ARMSTRONG. AMONG HIS MANY SONGS WAS "CALEDONIA" WHICH SWEPT THE NATION. (1940's)

36

EARL B. DICKERSON

IN 1955

HUMANITARIAN · LAWYER
BUSINESS EXECUTIVE

IN 1971

Geo LEE

IN 1978

ONE OF CHICAGO'S
DISTINGUISHED
BUSINESSMEN AND
FIGHTER OF CIVIL
RIGHTS. A BRILLIANT
ATTORNEY WHOSE LANDMARK VICTORY IN
THE 1940 U.S. SUPREME COURT DECISION IN
THE CASE OF HANSBERRY VS LEE THAT
OPENED UP RESTRICTED HOUSING TO
BLACKS. BORN IN CANTON, MISS., 1891. HIS
FATHER DIED WHEN HE WAS 4, MOTHER
TOOK IN WASHING. EARLY EDUCATION IN
CANTON AND NEW ORLEANS. IN 1907 WENT TO
CHICAGO FOR MORE SCHOOLING; HE HAD TO FIND
WORK. HE WASHED WINDOWS, SCRUBBED FLOORS,
BUSSED DISHES AND WORKED HIS WAY INTO NORTHWESTERN U., U OF ILL.,
(1914) AND RECEIVED HIS U OF CHICAGO LAW DEGREE (1920). IN 1921 HE
JOINED THE LIBERTY LIFE INS., CO (LATER SUPREME LIFE) AS GENERAL
COUNSEL. DURING WORLD WAR I HE SERVED AS 2nd LT., IN THE 365th
INFANTRY IN FRANCE; ONE OF THE FOUNDERS OF THE AMERICAN LEGION
(1919); ASS'T CORP, COUNSEL (1923); ASS'T ATTORNEY GENERAL (1933); ON
THE FIRST F E P C COMM., (1941); ACTIVE IN POLITICS; ELECTED PRESIDENT
OF SUPREME LIFE INS., (1955); BOARD CHAIRMAN (1971); RETIRED 1973.
RECIPIENT OF MANY HONORARY AWARDS. AT 86, STILL HONORARY BOARD
CHAIRMAN!

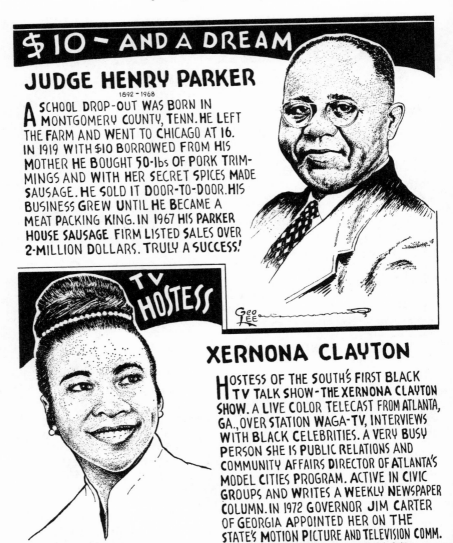

$10 - AND A DREAM

JUDGE HENRY PARKER
1892 - 1968

A SCHOOL DROP-OUT WAS BORN IN MONTGOMERY COUNTY, TENN. HE LEFT THE FARM AND WENT TO CHICAGO AT 16. IN 1919 WITH $10 BORROWED FROM HIS MOTHER HE BOUGHT 50-lbs OF PORK TRIMMINGS AND WITH HER SECRET SPICES MADE SAUSAGE. HE SOLD IT DOOR-TO-DOOR. HIS BUSINESS GREW UNTIL HE BECAME A MEAT PACKING KING. IN 1967 HIS PARKER HOUSE SAUSAGE FIRM LISTED SALES OVER 2-MILLION DOLLARS. TRULY A SUCCESS!

Geo Lee

TV HOSTESS

XERNONA CLAYTON

H OSTESS OF THE SOUTH'S FIRST BLACK TV TALK SHOW - THE XERNONA CLAYTON SHOW. A LIVE COLOR TELECAST FROM ATLANTA, GA., OVER STATION WAGA-TV, INTERVIEWS WITH BLACK CELEBRITIES. A VERY BUSY PERSON SHE IS PUBLIC RELATIONS AND COMMUNITY AFFAIRS DIRECTOR OF ATLANTA'S MODEL CITIES PROGRAM. ACTIVE IN CIVIC GROUPS AND WRITES A WEEKLY NEWSPAPER COLUMN. IN 1972 GOVERNOR JIM CARTER OF GEORGIA APPOINTED HER ON THE STATE'S MOTION PICTURE AND TELEVISION COMM.

WALTER WHITE
1893 – 1955

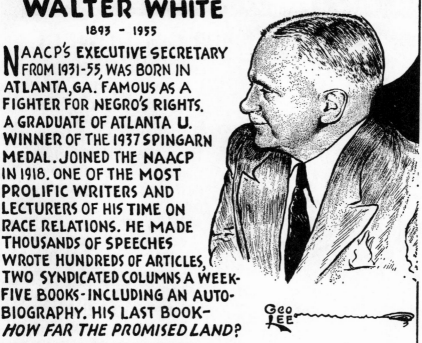

NAACP'S EXECUTIVE SECRETARY FROM 1931-55, WAS BORN IN ATLANTA, GA. FAMOUS AS A FIGHTER FOR NEGRO'S RIGHTS. A GRADUATE OF ATLANTA U. WINNER OF THE 1937 SPINGARN MEDAL. JOINED THE NAACP IN 1918. ONE OF THE MOST PROLIFIC WRITERS AND LECTURERS OF HIS TIME ON RACE RELATIONS. HE MADE THOUSANDS OF SPEECHES WROTE HUNDREDS OF ARTICLES, TWO SYNDICATED COLUMNS A WEEK- FIVE BOOKS-INCLUDING AN AUTO-BIOGRAPHY. HIS LAST BOOK- *HOW FAR THE PROMISED LAND?*

Geo Lee

JUST ANOTHER LUCKY NIGHT! — BLACKBURN

CHARLES HENRY (JACK) BLACKBURN
1883 – 1942

THE FINE TRAINER WHO GUIDED JOE LOUIS TO THE WORLD'S HEAVYWEIGHT CHAMPIONSHIP IN 1937, WAS A GREAT LIGHTWEIGHT. THE FIRST 8 YEARS OF HIS CAREER, HE WAS NEVER KNOCKED OFF HIS FEET-LOST ONLY ONCE TO CHAMP JOE GANS (15-RDS)'04

A BUSINESS ENTREPRENEUR

1894
1977

DR. C.B. POWELL

ONE OF THE NATION'S RICHEST BLACKS. A PUBLISHER, X-RAY SPECIALIST, CIVIC LEADER, BUSINESS ENTREPRENEUR AND HUMANITARIAN. HE LEFT NEARLY 3-MILLION TO HIS ALMA MATER, HOWARD U. BORN CLIFLAN BETHANY IN NEWPORT NEWS, VA. AT 15 HE WAS AN ORDERLY IN A LONG ISLAND(NY) HOSPITAL. WORKED HIS WAY THROUGH VA. NORMAL COLLEGE AND GRADUATED FROM HOWARD U. WITH A MEDICAL DEGREE (1920). INTERNED AT BELLEVUE HOSP,(NY) AND BECAME THE FIRST BLACK X-RAY SPECIALIST. HE OPENED HIS OWN X-RAY LABORATORY. HIS BEST

Geo LEE

CUSTOMER A DR. P.H.M SAVORY TURNED OUT TO BE HIS BUSINESS PARTNER. IN 1934 THEY TOOK OVER THE VICTORY LIFE INS. CO. (ILL). IN 1936 ACQUIRED THE TROUBLED AMSTERDAM NEWS(HARLEM)NEWSPAPER FOR 5,000, SOLD IT FOR 2-MILLION IN 1971. HE HAD A VARIETY OF SUCCESSFUL BUSINESSES.

FIRST BLACK BOXING COMMISSIONER OF NEW YORK, APPOINTED BY GOV. THOMAS E. DEWEY-AUG,1943. RE-APPOINTED JAN,1946. A VERY BUSY MAN!

1982 GEO L. LEE FEATURE SERVICE

BORN TO REBEL

DR. BENJAMIN E. MAYS

WHO ONCE WORKED AS A PULLMAN PORTER TO EARN MONEY FOR HIS EDUCATION AND ROSE TO BECOME PRESIDENT OF MOREHOUSE COLLEGE IN ATLANTA, GA., WAS BORN IN 1894 IN EPWORTH, S.C. A BRILLIANT STUDENT, HE RECEIVED HIS EARLY EDUCATION IN S.C. HIS BACHELOR'S DEGREE FROM BATES COLLEGE, IN MAINE (1920); MASTER'S (1925) AND PH.D. (1935) FROM U. OF CHICAGO. DURING THIS PERIOD HE TAUGHT MATH AT MOREHOUSE AND WAS EXEC-SECRETARY OF THE TAMPA, FLA., URBAN LEAGUE. AFTER HIS PH.D HE BECAME DEAN OF RELIGION AT HOWARD UNIV. IN 1940 HE RE-

WINNER OF THE 1971-DORIE MILLER "MEDAL OF HONOR"

PRESIDENT EMERITUS OF MOREHOUSE COLLEGE

28 HONORARY DOCTORATES

MORE-HOUSE

TURNED TO MOREHOUSE AS PRESIDENT AND SERVED FOR 27-YEARS. DR. MAYS WAS THE FIRST BLACK ELECTED VICE-PRES. OF THE FEDERAL COUNCIL OF CHURCHES OF CHRIST IN AMERICA. FIRST BLACK PRESIDENT OF ATLANTA'S BOARD OF EDUCATION. VERY ACTIVE AS A LECTURER. HIS AUTOBIOGRAPHY "BORN TO REBEL" WAS HIS 8TH BOOK. A PHI BETA KAPPA MEMBER HE IS ONE OF THE OUTSTANDING BLACK MEN IN AMERICA.

Geo LEE

41

CRYSTAL BIRD FAUSET FIRST

FIRST BLACK WOMAN TO SERVE IN A STATE LEGISLATURE. THE BOSTON-BRED LEGISLATOR MADE HER MARK IN THE GREAT GAME OF POLITICS IN 1938...WHEN SHE WAS DULY ELECTED TO THE HOUSE OF REPRESENTATIVES OF THE STATE OF PENNSYLVANIA(D). IN 1939 GOV. GEORGE H. EARLE CITED HER WITH THE MERITORIOUS SERVICE MEDAL OF PA. (DIED '65)

CORA M. BROWN

FIRST BLACK WOMAN IN THE NATION TO BE ELECTED A STATE SENATOR IN 1952 FROM THE... STATE OF MICHIGAN. THE DETROIT ATTORNEY WAS A SOCIAL WORKER BEFORE RECEIVING HER LAW DEGREE. A VERY AGGRESSIVE LEGISLATOR SHE EARNED THE LABEL :.."CHAMPION OF THE UNDERPRIVILEGED." SENATOR BROWN LATER BECAME A PRACTICING ATTORNEY LIVING IN LOS ANGELES.

GEO LEE

BEULAH

SHE WAS THE 13TH CHILD IN HER FAMILY.

THE LOVABLE RADIO CHARACTER PLAYED BY HATTIE, THE FIRST BLACK ACTRESS TO HAVE HER OWN COAST-TO-COAST RADIO SHOW.(1947) "BEULAH"

HATTIE STARTED HER CAREER SINGING WITH A BAND AND TOURED THE VAUDEVILLE CIRCUITS. LATER SHE HEADED FOR HOLLYWOOD AND THE MOVIES...

"CALIFORNIA, HERE I COME"

Geo LEE

HOLLYWOOD 10 MI

....ARRIVED IN HOLLYWOOD WITH ONLY -$20.

HATTIE McDANIEL
1895 - 1952

BORN IN WICHITA, KAN. AT THE AGE OF TWO HER FAMILY MOVED TO DENVER, COLO., WHERE SHE RECEIVED HER EARLY EDUCATION. HER FATHER WAS A BAPTIST MINISTER AND SHE SANG AS A CHILD IN THE CHURCH CHOIR. WHEN SHE WAS A TEENAGER SHE WON A MEDAL FOR HER RECITATION OF "CONVICT JOE." IT WAS HER FIRST DRAMATIC EFFORT. ALTHO SHE WAS THE FIRST BLACK TO WIN AN "OSCAR" FOR HER ROLE IN "GONE WITH THE WIND"(1939), SHE WAS OFTEN CRITICIZED FOR THE ROLES SHE PLAYED.

1973 George L. Lee Feature Service

43

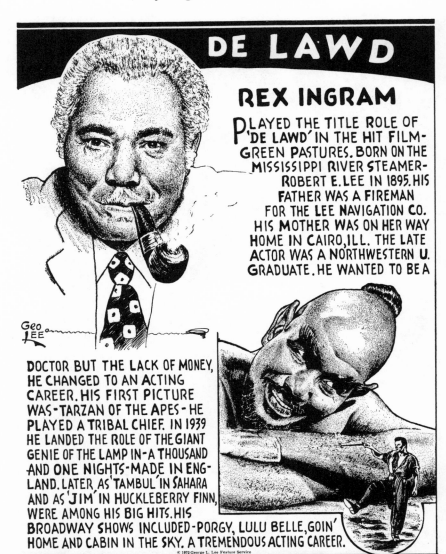

DE LAWD

REX INGRAM

PLAYED THE TITLE ROLE OF 'DE LAWD' IN THE HIT FILM- GREEN PASTURES. BORN ON THE MISSISSIPPI RIVER STEAMER- ROBERT E. LEE IN 1895. HIS FATHER WAS A FIREMAN FOR THE LEE NAVIGATION CO. HIS MOTHER WAS ON HER WAY HOME IN CAIRO, ILL. THE LATE ACTOR WAS A NORTHWESTERN U. GRADUATE. HE WANTED TO BE A

Geo LEE

DOCTOR BUT THE LACK OF MONEY, HE CHANGED TO AN ACTING CAREER. HIS FIRST PICTURE WAS-TARZAN OF THE APES- HE PLAYED A TRIBAL CHIEF. IN 1939 HE LANDED THE ROLE OF THE GIANT GENIE OF THE LAMP IN-A THOUSAND AND ONE NIGHTS-MADE IN ENG- LAND. LATER, AS 'TAMBUL' IN SAHARA AND AS 'JIM' IN HUCKLEBERRY FINN, WERE AMONG HIS BIG HITS. HIS BROADWAY SHOWS INCLUDED-PORGY, LULU BELLE, GOIN' HOME AND CABIN IN THE SKY. A TREMENDOUS ACTING CAREER.

© 1972 George L. Lee Feature Service

44

'HIS EYE IS ON THE SPARROW'

ETHEL WATERS

1. THE INCOMPARABLE, WAS BORN IN CHESTER, PA., IN 1900. A GREAT CAREER WAS STARTED AT **17**, AS A BLUES SINGER. SHE WAS THE FIRST WOMAN TO SING THE "ST. LOUIS BLUES. HER EARLY YEARS WERE IN VAUDEVILLE, CARNIVALS AND MISTY NIGHT CLUBS. A ONE-WEEK ENGAGEMENT AT THE OLD LINCOLN THEATER IN HARLEM LED TO BIGGER THINGS – THE PLANTATION CLUB ON BROADWAY IN 1923.

AS THOUSANDS CHEER - 1933

MAMBA'S DAUGHTER 1939

CABIN IN THE SKY - 1940

BLUE HOLIDAY - 1945

THE MEMBER OF THE WEDDING 1951

AT HOME WITH ETHEL WATERS 1953

PINKY

AT HOME ABROAD

DIED 1977

HER AUTOBIOGRAPHY – HIS EYE IS ON THE SPARROW – WAS A BEST-SELLER....

Geo Lee

2. HER RECORDINGS SOON REACHED THE MASSES AND HER STAR SHONE BRIGHTLY. SHE APPEARED ON BROADWAY IN, "AS THOUSANDS CHEER", A MUSICAL. HER ABILITY AS AN ACTRESS WAS APPARENT AS – HAGAR – IN "MAMBA'S DAUGHTER". IN 1939 SHE SANG IN CARNEGIE HALL.

3. HOLLYWOOD BECKONED AND FILMS –"CABIN IN THE SKY" AND "PINKY" AMONG THEM. FOR HER ROLE IN, "THE MEMBER OF THE WEDDING," (1951) SHE WON THE N.Y. DRAMA CRITICS AWARD. IN 1957 SHE ATTENDED A BILLY GRAHAM CRUSADE IN N.Y.C., TRULY INSPIRED SHE ACCEPTED A CHANCE TO SING. AT THE AGE OF 72-YEARS SHE STILL SINGS TO GOD, ON THE CRUSADE.

45

NATION of ISLAM-LEADER

HON. ELIJAH MUHAMMAD
1897 - 1975

WHO ROSE FROM A LABORER TO THE MILLIONAIRE LEADER OF THE NATION OF ISLAM, ALSO KNOWN AS THE BLACK MUSLIMS.... A RELIGIOUS ORGANIZATION. BORN ELIJAH POOLE, ONE OF 13 IN SANDERSVILLE, GA. HIS FATHER A BAPTIST PREACHER AND SHARECROPPER. ELIJAH HAD TO QUIT SCHOOL IN THE FOURTH GRADE TO WORK. HIS SISTER TAUGHT HIM TO READ AND WRITE. HE SPENT HOURS READING THE BIBLE. IN 1919, MARRIED

CLEAN LIVING, NATIONAL BANK, FISH IMPORTS, SELF-RESPECT, CLOTHING, RESTAURANTS, CATTLE, CLEAN LIVING, PRIDE, FARMS, FLEET OF TRUCKS, SELF-UPLIFT, BAKERIES, NEWSPAPER, SCHOOLS

KNOWN AS THE "MESSENGER" THE NATION GREW AND BECAME A FINANCIAL SUCCESS.

Geo Lee

CLARA EVANS. IN 1923 THEY MOVED TO DETROIT WITH TWO CHILDREN... LATER EIGHT. IN 1930 MET A W.D. FARD A SELF-IMPOSED PROPHET WHO HAD A FOLLOWING. ELIJAH JOINED AND BECAME KNOWN AS "ELIJAH MUHAMMAD." THEY WERE CO-FOUNDERS OF THE.... NATION OF ISLAM IN DETROIT, LATER IN CHICAGO. FARD DROPPED OUT AND ELIJAH ASSUMED LEADERSHIP IN 1934.

1978 Geo L. Lee Feature Serv

HISTORIAN · EDUCATOR

DR. RAYFORD W. LOGAN

PROFESSOR EMERITUS OF HISTORY AT HOWARD U. HIS STRENUOUS EFFORTS TO ENLIGHTEN THE WORLD ABOUT THE BLACKs AND THEIR CONTRIBUTIONS TO AMERICA. BORN IN WASH,D.C.,JAN 7, 1897. EARLY EDUCATION IN SEGREGATED PUBLIC SCHOOLS. A BRILLIANT STUDENT... A PHI BETA KAPPA GRADUATE OF WILLIAMS COLLEGE (MASS) IN 1917... WORKING HIS WAY. SERVED AS AN OFFICER IN WORLD WAR I IN FRANCE AND SAW THE RACISM IN THE U.S. ARMY... DISCHARGED,1919 AND STAYED IN FRANCE FOR 5-YEARS. HE MET DR.DuBOIS THERE WHO HAD FOUNDED THE PAN-AFRICAN CONGRESS (1921).

65th SPINGARN MEDAL WINNER! NAACP'S HIGHEST ACHIEVEMENT AWARD TO AN AMERICAN BLACK (1980) AUTHOR OF 14 BOOKS, 115 PUBLICATIONS. HIS CONTRIBUTIONS WERE GREAT! DR.LOGAN DIED AT 85...(1982).

LOGAN BECAME ACTIVE AS A COLLABORATOR. HE RETURNED TO D.C. (1924). TAUGHT AT VIRGINIA UNION 1925-30. WENT TO HARVARD ON A FELLOWSHIP, EARNED A.M. IN HISTORY('32),PH.D ('36). TAUGHT AT ATLANTA U.1933-38, AND HOWARD U., AS PROFESSOR OF HISTORY, DEPT. HEAD FROM 1938 UNTIL HE RETIRED,1965...APPOINTED DISTINGUISHED PROFESSOR OF HISTORY IN 1971!

1984 Geo L, Lee Feature Service

1898. 1974 BRILLIANT JUDGE

RAYMOND PACE ALEXANDER

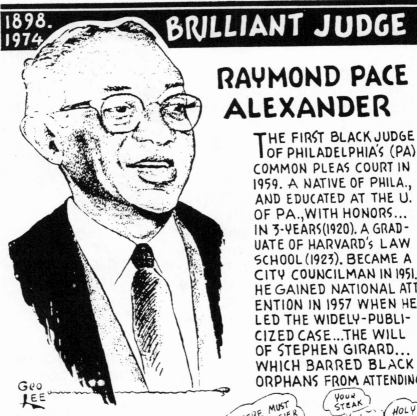

THE FIRST BLACK JUDGE OF PHILADELPHIA'S (PA) COMMON PLEAS COURT IN 1959. A NATIVE OF PHILA., AND EDUCATED AT THE U. OF PA., WITH HONORS... IN 3-YEARS (1920). A GRADUATE OF HARVARD'S LAW SCHOOL (1923). BECAME A CITY COUNCILMAN IN 1951. HE GAINED NATIONAL ATTENTION IN 1957 WHEN HE LED THE WIDELY-PUBLICIZED CASE...THE WILL OF STEPHEN GIRARD... WHICH BARRED BLACK ORPHANS FROM ATTENDING

Geo LEE

PHILADELPHIA'S GIRARD COLLEGE. HE WENT ALL-THE-WAY TO THE SUPREME COURT AND WON! A PIONEER IN THE FIGHT FOR CIVIL-RIGHTS. IN HIS EARLY DAYS HE WORKED AS A RED CAP AND A PULLMAN CAR COOK!

THERE MUST BE AN EASIER WAY TO MAKE A LIVING

YOUR STEAK

HOLY SMOKE WHAT'S THAT?

DR. HOWARD THURMAN

NOTED THEOLOGIAN AND DEAN EMERITUS OF THE MARSH CHAPEL OF BOSTON UNIV., WAS AWARDED THE 1968 GUTENBERG AWARD FOR HIS ACHIEVEMENTS IN RELIGION AND EDUCATION. THE FLORIDA-BORN GRANDSON OF A SLAVE, PRESSED PANTS TO GET THRU SCHOOL. A GRADUATE OF MOREHOUSE COLLEGE HE BEGAN HIS CAREER AS PASTOR OF MT. ZION BAPTIST CHURCH IN OBERLIN, OHIO IN 1926. IN 1944 HE ORGANIZED AND WAS THE FIRST MINISTER OF THE FIRST INTEGRATED CHURCH IN THE U.S... THE FELLOWSHIP CHURCH FOR ALL PEOPLES... IN SAN FRANCISCO. LIFE

1900-1981

MAGAZINE IN 1953 SELECTED THE BAPTIST MINISTER AS ONE OF 12 "GREAT PREACHERS" OF THIS CENTURY. NOW RETIRED,(1971) HE HEADS THE HOWARD THURMAN EDUCATIONAL TRUST.

1882 1949

FIRST

FERDINAND Q. MORTON

THE FIRST BLACK TO BE APPOINTED ON THE N.Y. CIVIL SERVICE COMMISSION, AND SERVED 24-YEARS BEFORE HE BECAME PRESIDENT OF THE COMMISSION IN 1946. BORN IN MISSISSIPPI HE SPENT HIS EARLY YEARS IN WASH., D.C. HE WORKED HIS WAY THRU HARVARD AND BOSTON LAW SCHOOL BY WAITING ON TABLES!

GeoLee

ROY WILKINS
EXECUTIVE DIRECTOR-NAACP

JOINED THE STAFF OF THE NAACP IN 1931 AS ASS'T EXECUTIVE SECRETARY. HE SUCCEEDED WALTER WHITE AS SECRETARY IN 1955. AN EX-NEWSPAPERMAN, HE WAS ONCE EDITOR OF THE 'CALL' IN KANSAS CITY. WON THE 49th SPINGARN MEDAL FOR DISTINGUISHED ACHIEVEMENT IN 1964. RECEIVED EIGHT HONORARY DEGREES IN 1965. AWARDED THE 1967 FREEDOM AWARD FOR HIS **UNTIRING** EFFORTS IN **CIVIL RIGHTS.**

Geo Lee

HE FOUNDED A TOWN!

ISAIAH T. MONTGOMERY

WAS BORN A SLAVE ON THE PLANTATION OF JOSEPH DAVIS, BROTHER OF JEFF DAVIS THE "PRESIDENT OF THE CONFEDERACY"ON MAY 21,1847, NEAR VICKSBURG, MISS. EDUCATED BY HIS PARENTS, HE ROSE TO FOUND AND PLAN THE ALL-NEGRO TOWN-MOUND BAYOU, MISS. THE FIRST SURVEY IN JULY 1887. FIRST SETTLERS IN 1888.

LOOKIN' BACK TO RADIO

AMANDA RANDOLPH

STAGE AND RADIO ACTRESS WHO PLAYED COMEDY AND SERIOUS ROLES. FOR MANY YEARS SHE SENT SHIVERS AND LAUGHTER UP THE SPINES OF MILLIONS AS THE CANT- ANKEROUS MOTHER-IN-LAW OF "KINGFISH" ON THE AMOS 'N' ANDY SHOW. BORN IN LOUISVILLE, KY., SHE ATTENDED SCHOOL IN CLEVELAND, OH. HER CAREER BEGAN IN CINCINNATI AND SHE WAS INVITED TO JOIN THE STAGE SHOW "SHUFFLE ALONG" IN N.Y., IN 1924. TOURED EUROPE IN A VARIETY ACT FOR 9-MONTHS IN 1930. ON HER RETURN, WORKED IN VAUDE-

Geo Lee

AMANDA PLAYED "VENUS GEETCH" THE 200-POUND HOUSEKEEPER ON THE "MISS HATTIE" SHOW, STARRING ETHEL BARRY- MORE AND AIR- ED SUNDAYS OVER WJZ (NYC) 1945. SHE AND ETHEL.... PLAYED VAUDEVILLE AND ONCE ON THE SAME BILL IN 1932.

VILLE. RECEIVED A CHOICE ROLE IN THE SMASH HIT, "THE MALE ANI- MAL". SHE STARTED WORKING IN RADIO SHOWS AND PLAYED "LILLY" IN THE RADIO SERIAL "ABIE'S IRISH ROSE" FOR NEARLY 2-YEARS. APPEARED FOR 11-YEARS AS THE MAID ON THE "DANNY THOMAS" TV SHOW BEFORE SHE RETIRED. AMANDA DIED AT 65 IN 1967.

1984 Geo L. Lee Feature Service

LOOKING BACK TO THE FORTIES

DR. WILLIAM J. KNOX

THE DISTINGUISHED CHEMIST WHOSE VALUABLE EFFORTS AIDED THE "MANHATTAN PROJECT" WHEN HE WAS ASSIGNED IN DECEMBER, 1942. THE ATOM BOMB PROJECT WAS LOCATED AT COLUMBIA UNIV., N.Y.C. DR. KNOX EARNED HIS B.S. IN CHEMISTRY FROM HARVARD UNIV., HIS MASTERS AND PH.D FROM M.I.T. (MASS.) A SENIOR MEMBER OF THE NAT'L DEFENSE RESEARCH COMM. HE ONCE TAUGHT CHEMISTRY AT HOWARD AND ATLANTA UNIVERSITIES.

1942

GWENDOLYN BROOKS

1945

THE CHICAGO GIRL WHO STARTED WRITING POETRY AT THE AGE OF 7-YEARS WAS CHOSEN ONE OF MADEMO-ISELLE MAGAZINE'S 10 "WOMEN OF THE YEAR" AWARDS IN 1945... FOR HER WIDELY ACCLAIMED FIRST BOOK OF POEMS "A STREET IN BRONZEVILLE."

1946

HELEN MARIE GUENVEUR

NEXT!

BOY! OH BOY! A LADY DENTIST!

OF CHARLESTON, S.C., WHO GRADUATED FROM THE MEHARRY DENTAL SCHOOL IN 1946, TOPPED HER CLASS FOR HONORS: SHE WON THE SCHOLASTIC ACHIEVEMENT AWARD - THE AMERICAN SOCIETY OF DENTISTRY FOR CHILDREN AWARD - THE OLIVER GOLD MEDAL FOR EXCELLENCE IN CLINICAL DEN-TISTRY AND HAD THE HIGHEST GRADES FOR 4-YEARS!

Geo. Lee

NOTED SOCIAL ANTHROPOLOGIST

DR. ALLISON DAVIS

BRILLIANT EDUCATOR WHO RE-SEARCHED THE DIFFERENCES OF BLACK CHILDREN OF THE RURAL SOUTH AND THE URBAN NORTH. HE SOUGHT TO RE-EVALUATE IQ TESTS FOR POOR CHILDREN. HIS ANTHROPOLOGY STUDIES WERE HIGHLY SIGNIFICANT. BORN OCT. 14,1902 IN WASH., D.C. HE RECEIVED HIS A.B. AT WILLIAMS COLLEGE GRADUATING, SUMMA CUM LAUDE, VALEDICTORIAN (1924); M.A. FROM HARVARD UNIV.,1925; AWARDED ROSEN-WALD FELLOWSHIP FOR FOREIGN STUDY AT LONDON SCHOOL OF ECONOMICS (1932-33); GRADUATE STUDY AT U OF CHICAGO, 1939-40 (ROSENWALD FELLOWSHIP); PH.D

Geo LEE

AUTHOR OR CO-AUTHOR OF 10-BOOKS OF RESEA-RCH ON BLACK AMER-ICA... THE SOCIAL PRE-SSURES THEY ENDURE TO MAINTAIN THEIR PRIDE, IDENTITY AND COMPETENCE. HIS BOOKS AIDED HEAD-START PROGRAMS!

1984 Geo L. Lee Feature Service

AT CHICAGO,1941. THE FIRST BLACK PROFESSOR AT U OF CHICAGO,1942. AT THE TIME OF HIS DEATH NOV 23,1983, HE HELD THE POSITION OF JOHN DEWEY DISTINGUISHED SERVICE PROFESSOR IN EDUCATION. A PIONEER IN BLACK AMERICA STUDY.

ZORA NEALE HURSTON
1903 – 1960

ONE OF THE MOST PROLIFIC WRITERS OF HER ERA. AN AUTHORITY ON NEGRO FOLKLORE AND ANTHROPOLOGY. BORN EATONVILLE, FLA. SHE ATTENDED HIGH SCHOOL AT MORGAN ACADEMY OF MORGAN COLLEGE, BALTIMORE. EARNED HER B.A. FROM BARNARD COLLEGE IN 1928. WAS GRANTED A FELLOWSHIP IN ANTHROPOLOGY TO RESEARCH IN FOLKLORE. AFTER 4-YEARS IN THIS FIELD WAS INVITED TO JOIN THE AMERICAN FOLKLORE SOCIETY, AMERICAN ETHNOLOGICAL SOCIETY AND ANTHROPOLOGICAL SOCIETY. MISS. HURSTON DECIDED TO BECOME A WRITER AND "WRITE" ABOUT HER PEOPLE. SHE RECEIVED FELLOWSHIPS FROM THE ROSENWALD FOUNDATION (1935) AND GUGGENHEIM (1935 AND 1936). AMONG HER BOOKS - 'JONAH'S GOURD VINE,' 1934; 'MULES AND MEN,' 1936; 'THEIR EYES WERE WATCHING GOD,' 1937. HER AUTOBIOGRAPHY - 'DUST TRACKS ON THE ROAD,' 1942, WON ANNISFIELD AWARD.

Geo Lee

ARNA BONTEMPS
1902 – 1973

POET, AUTHOR AND LIBRARIAN OF FISK UNIV., FOR 22-YEARS... ONCE CO-AUTHORED THE BROADWAY MUSICAL COMEDY HIT, "ST LOUIS WOMAN" WITH COUNTEE CULLEN. HE FIRST WROTE THE PLOT IN HIS NOVEL "GOD SENDS SUNDAY," IN 1931. BORN IN ALEXANDRIA, LA. HIS EARLY YEARS WERE SPENT IN CALIF., WHERE HE RECEIVED MOST OF HIS EDUCATION. EARNED HIS M.A. IN ENGLISH LITERATURE FROM THE U OF CHICAGO. HIS - "STORY OF THE NEGRO," WON THE JANE ADDAMS CHILDREN'S BOOK AWARD FOR 1956. WROTE OVER 10 BOOKS FOR BLACK JUVENILES. WON MANY AWARDS INCLUDING - THE ALEXANDER PUSHKIN POETRY PRIZE (1926-27). COMPILED AN ANTHOLOGY OF NEGRO POETRY, "GOLDEN SLIPPERS."
(1941)

MEDICAL WRITER

DR. W. MONTAGUE COBB

DISTINGUISHED PROFESSOR OF ANATOMY AT HOWARD U., TAUGHT 38-YEARS AS A PROFESSOR AND HEAD OF THE DEPARTMENT OF ANATOMY. HE WAS BORN IN WASH. D.C. IN 1904 WHERE HE GRADUATED FROM DUNBAR HI. DR. COBB RECEIVED HIS A.B. DEGREE FROM AMHERST COLLEGE (1925), M.D. DEGREE AT HOWARD U. (1929) AND PH.D. WESTERN RESERVE U., (1932). BRILLIANT IN HIS FIELD HE IS A MEDICAL WRITER OF NOTE, AN EDITOR, HISTORIAN AND A PIONEER CIVIL RIGHTS ACTIVIST. IN 1964-65 HE WAS PRESIDENT OF THE NATIONAL MEDICAL ASSOC., AND HAS BEEN EDITOR OF ITS JOURNAL SINCE 1949. HE SERVED ON THE BOARD OF DIRECTORS AND ON THE PROFESSIONAL EDUCATION COMM. OF THE AMERICAN HEART ASSOC., A MEMBER OF THE AMERICAN ASSOC. OF ANATOMISTS; AMERICAN ASSOC. FOR THE HISTORY OF MEDICINE, TO NAME A FEW. HE LED THE FIGHT FOR THE ADMISSION OF BLACK PHYSICIANS TO THE D.C. GENERAL HOSPITAL AND THE D.C. MEDICAL SOCIETY. A LIFE MEMBER AND A BOARD MEMBER OF THE NAACP.

Geo
Lee

EMPEROR HAILE SELASSIE I

OF ETHIOPIA WAS BORN LIJ TAFARI MAKONNEN IN THE REGION OF HARAR (THE LAND OF THE QUEEN OF SHEBA) IN 1892. A DESCENDANT OF THE RULERS, 11-CENTURIES BEFORE CHRIST. HE ASSUMED THE THRONE IN 1930 AND IN 1936 THE ITALIANS UNDER MUSSOLINI INVADED. ALTHOUGH HE WAS A MEMBER OF THE LEAGUE OF NATIONS... THEY FAILED TO ACT. SELASSIE PROPHESIED THAT A WORLD WAR WOULD BE THE RESULT OF THEIR FAILURE-HE WAS RIGHT. IN 1941, HE REGAINED HIS THRONE.

1892–1975

TOP CRIMINAL LAWYER

MAJOR EUCLID LOUIS TAYLOR
1905-1970

WHO ONCE WON OVER 150 CONSECUTIVE COURTROOM VICTORIES, WAS THE FIRST BLACK APPOINTED TO THE CHICAGO STATE'S ATTORNEY'S OFFICE AND THE YOUNGEST MAN...ONLY 24-YEARS OLD. BORN IN COFFEYVILLE, KAN., HE WENT TO CHICAGO WHERE HE WORKED NIGHTS AS A POSTAL CLERK TO EARN TUITION TO LAW SCHOOL. AFTER HIS ASS'T STATE'S ATTORNEY DUTIES HE WENT INTO PRIVATE PRACTICE. HIS RISE WAS RAPID. TAYLOR SOON FOUND FAME AS THE NATION'S TOP CRIMINAL LAWYER. IN 1947 HE RECEIVED HIS CERTIFICATE OF ADMISSION TO PRACTICE BEFORE THE U.S. SUPREME COURT. TAUGHT AT JOHN MARSHALL LAW SCHOOL. HIS EXTRADITION PAPERS THAT BROUGHT SAMUEL INSULL, ONCE HEAD OF AN EMPIRE...BACK TO THE U.S. FROM GREECE ON LARCENY AND EMBEZZLEMENT CHARGES...WAS A GEM!

Geo LEE

BUD BILLIKEN

DAVID W. KELLUM

FORMER CITY EDITOR OF THE CHICAGO DAILY DEFENDER AND CREATOR OF THE "BUD BILLIKEN PARADE" AND PICNIC. IT STARTED ON THE FIRST SATURDAY OF AUGUST 1929. A NATIVE OF GREENVILLE, MISS., GRADUATED FROM THE WENDELL PHILLIPS HIGH SCHOOL IN CHICAGO AND WAS THE FIRST BLACK STUDENT TO BE COMMISSIONED A CADET MAJOR IN THE PUBLIC SCHOOLS' RESERVE OFFICERS TRAINING CORPS. HE WAS

Geo Lee — DIED 1981

BUD BILLIKEN

HI BUD!

HI BUD!

DAVE MADE THE "BUD BILLIKEN CLUB" INTO A NATIONAL INSTITUTION .....

COMMISSIONED A 2nd LT., IN THE ILL. NATIONAL GUARD (BREVET) BY GOV. LEN SMALL. ATTENDED THE MEDILL SCHOOL OF JOURNALISM OF NORTHWESTERN UNIV. KELLUM JOINED THE CHICAGO DEFENDER STAFF IN 1923 AS A COPY-BOY AND MOVED-UP TO EDITOR OF THE JUNIOR PAGE AND

SPENT 26-YEARS INSPIRING YOUTH... LATER CITY EDITOR.

1979   GEO L. LEE FEATURE SERVICE

FROM DOOR TO DOOR TO SUCCESS

S. B. FULLER

AN OUTSTANDING BUSINESSMAN WHO OPENED THE DOOR FOR THOUSANDS OF BLACK PEOPLE FOR SELF-HELP WITH HIS DOOR-TO-DOOR DIRECT SELLING. BORN ON A LOUISIANA FARM NEAR MONROE IN 1905. HIS SCHOOLING WAS LIMITED...ONLY THE SIXTH GRADE. HE WENT TO WORK. ORPHANED AT 17, HE WAS THE SOLE SUPPORT OF 7 YOUNGER BROTHERS AND SISTERS. IN 1928, HITCH-HIKED FROM MEMPHIS TO CHICAGO. WORKED IN A COALYARD, INS. AGENT, LATER A MANAGER.

Geo LEE

IN 1935 HE REALIZED THE POTENTIAL IN BLACK BUSINESS IN THE COSMETICS FIELD. WITH $25 – HE BOUGHT SOME SOAP AND WENT

MY PRODUCTS ARE GOOD AND THEY WILL SELL

MR. FULLER, THE MASTER SALESMAN, WAS ABLE TO TEACH HIS METHODS TO SALES MEN AND WOMEN WHO NEVER DREAMED OF SUCH EARNINGS!

DOOR TO DOOR SELLING AND NEVER STOPPED. HE FOUNDED THE FULLER PRODUCTS CO. DURING THE 1940s AND 1950s FULLER BECAME A NATIONAL PHENOMENON...WITH 5-SUBSIDIARIES, A MULTI-MILLION GROSS INCOME AND BRANCH OFFICES IN EVERY MAJOR CITY IN THE U.S. A TREMENDOUS INSPIRATION AND BUSINESS PIONEER!

1981 GEO L. LEE FEATURE SERVICE

"NEW WORLD A-COMING"

ROI OTTLEY
1906 – 1960

NOTED AUTHOR AND JOURNALIST WHOSE FIRST BOOK IN 1943 – "NEW WORLD A-COMING" BECAME A BEST-SELLER AND WON THE AINSWORTH AWARD AND THE "LIFE IN AMERICA" AWARD. BORN IN N.Y.C. HE WAS EDUCATED AT ST. BON-AVENTURE; U OF MICH; AND ST. JOHN'S LAW SCHOOL. A STAR ATHLETE, HE STARTED HIS CAREER AS A REPORTER ON THE N.Y. AMSTERDAM STAR NEWS. HE WAS THE FIRST BLACK WAR CORRESPONDENT ON A WHITE DAILY (N.Y. PM). HIS RADIO INTERVIEW PROGRAM WAS AIRED OVER WGN CHICAGO.

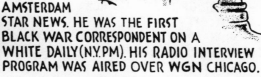

MADAME EVANTI

THE LATE WORLD FAMOUS OPERA SINGER, WHOSE REAL NAME – LILLIAN EVANS TIBBS, STARTED HER MUSICAL TRAINING AT 4 AND WAS A CHILD PIANO PRODIGY. AN HONOR GRADUATE OF HOWARD U. – STUDIED IN EUROPE. MADE HER DEBUT IN 1925 IN NICE, FRANCE. SANG IN THE CAPITOLS OF EUROPE AND SO. AMERICA. A FOUNDER OF THE NEGRO NATIONAL OPERA CO. ALTHO BARRED FROM THE "MET" (1932), SHE GAVE CONCERTS IN U.S.

Geo LEE

© 1974 George L. Lee Feature Service

59

TED POSTON
1906 - 1974

ONE THE MOST PROLIFIC NEWSPAPERMEN OF HIS TIME. BORN IN HOPKINS- VILLE, KY., ON JULY 4. HE RECEIVED HIS HIGHER ED- UCATION FROM TENNESSEE STATE COLLEGE, GRADUATING IN 1928. TED DID GRADUATE WORK AT NEW YORK UNIV., IN EDITORIAL AND SHORT- STORY WRITING. HE ENTERED THE NEWSPAPER FIELD.... SERVED AS MANAGING ED- ITOR OF THE N.Y. CONTENDER; N.Y. EDITOR OF THE PITTSBURGH COURIER; CITY EDITOR OF THE NEW YORK AMSTERDAM- STAR NEWS AND FEATURE WRITER, REPORTER AND CHIEF REWRITE MAN FOR THE NEW YORK POST FOR OVER 30- YEARS. IN 1940 HE SERVED AS PUBLIC-RELATIONS CON- SULTANT FOR THE NATIONAL ADVISORY DEFENSE COMMISSION; ALSO FOR THE WAR MAN POWER COMM. IN 1940 WAS CHIEF OF THE NEGRO NEWS DESK IN THE NEWS BUREAU, OFFICE OF WAR INFORMATION. HIGHLY RESPECTED BY BLACK JOURNALISTS HE WAS KNOWN AS THE "DEAN OF BLACK JOURNALISTS."

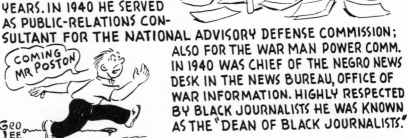

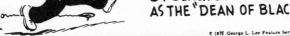

© 1975 George L. Lee Feature Service

CUTIE – THE GLAMOROUS RED HEADED CARTOON GIRL WAS CREATED BY E. SIMMS CAMPBELL. ONE OF AMERICA'S TOP CARTOONISTS. HE STARTED HIS CAREER WHEN HE RECEIVED 75¢ FOR A DRAWING OF A TURKEY.

E. SIMMS CAMPBELL
1906 – 1971

WHO HAD A DEGREE FROM THE CHICAGO ART INSTITUTE – BUT THE COLOR-LINE WAS SO GREAT HE HAD TO TAKE A JOB AS A DINING CAR WAITER. HE SENT HIS CARTOONS TO TOP MAGAZINES. THEY WERE ACCEPTED. IN 1933 HE STARTED WITH ESQUIRE AND BECAME A SUCCESS. HE CREATED "CUTIES", A SYNDICATED NEWSPAPER CARTOON THAT APPEARED IN 48 PAPERS. HIS HIGHLY HUMOROUS CARTOONS APPEARED IN PLAYBOY, LIFE, SATURDAY EVENING POST AND OTHERS. HE LIVED HIS LATTER LIFE IN SWITZERLAND BUT DIED IN N.Y.C. A BRILLIANT TALENT.

WITH APOLOGIES TO E. SIMMS CAMPBELL

GEO. LEE

CANADA LEE

1907 - 1952

THE DISTINGUISHED ACTOR OF THE BROADWAY STAGE, SCREEN AND RADIO WHO ROSE TO FAME WHEN HE PLAYED "BIGGER THOMAS" IN THE PLAY "NATIVE SON"(1941) WAS ONCE A LEADING CONTENDER FOR THE WELTERWEIGHT CROWN. AT SEVEN HE STUDIED THE VIOLIN UNDER J. ROSAMOND JOHNSON. AT 14 HE RAN OFF TO THE RACES AND BECAME A JOCKEY AT SARATOGA AND OTHER NEW YORK TRACKS. BUT WITH LITTLE SUCCESS HE TURNED TO BOXING. BORN LEONARD LIONEL CORNELIUS CANEGATA ON MAY 3, IN MANHATTAN'S SAN JUAN HILL DISTRICT AND WENT TO SCHOOL IN HARLEM. CANADA QUIT THE RING IN 1933. AFTER A **BLOW** DETACHED A RETINA IN HIS LEFT EYE DURING A BOUT IN 1929, HE CONTINUED ON DESPITE THE LOSS OF ONE EYE. HIS ACTING CAREER STARTED BY ACCIDENT. ONE DAY WHILE WALKING IN HARLEM HE DROPPED INTO THE "Y", THEY WERE CASTING FOR THE PLAY "BROTHER MOSES". HE READ FOR A PART AND GOT IT. A GREAT ACTING CAREER WAS BORN.

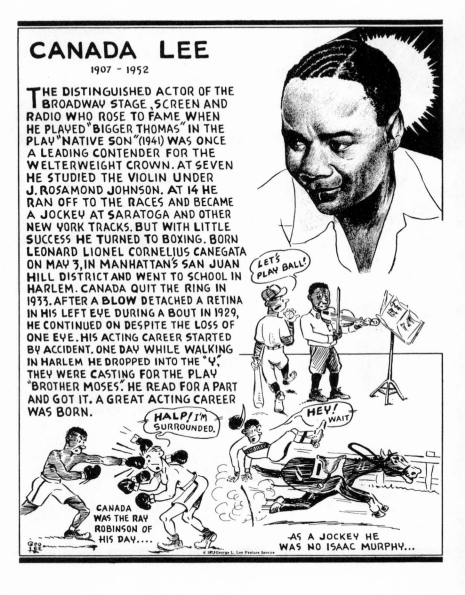

LET'S PLAY BALL!

HALP! I'M SURROUNDED.

HEY! WAIT

CANADA WAS THE RAY ROBINSON OF HIS DAY....

-AS A JOCKEY HE WAS NO ISAAC MURPHY...

© 1983 George L. Lee Feature Service

KING OF *HI·DE·HO*

CAB CALLOWAY
BORN IN ROCHESTER, N.Y.

WHO STARTED OUT TO BE A LAWYER AND RECEIVED HIS DEGREE AT CRANE COLLEGE, CHICAGO MADE HIS FIRST DEBUT AS A BANDLEADER IN THE FAMOUS "SUNSET CAFE" IN CHICAGO. WHILE ON THE AIR ONE NIGHT HE FORGOT THE WORDS—AND SCAT-SINGING WAS BORN. HE WAS EDUCATED IN BALTIMORE. HIS FAME STARTED IN 1931. CAB'S FIRST BROAD-WAY SHOW WAS "CONNIE'S HOT CHOCOLATES." HE STARRED IN HARLEM'S COTTON CLUB. IN 1952 TO '54, HE PLAYED THE

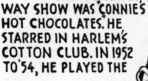

ROLE OF-SPORTIN' LIFE IN "PORGY AND BESS." LATER IN "THE BIG BROADCAST" SERIES, AND IN THE MOVIES IN-"THE SINGING KID," WITH AL JOLSON. ALSO "STORMY WEATHER", "ST. LOUIS BLUES" AND "THE CINCINNATI KID." AFTER MANY YEARS OF TV AND SINGING ALL OVER THE WORLD HE JOINED PEARL BAILEY IN THE CAST OF "OH DOLLY." AT 61 HE MADE A BRILLIANT COME-BACK, AS-HORACE VANDERGELDER. ONE OF THE GREATS IN $HOW *BIZ!*

FIRST BLACK IN U.S. CABINET

ROBERT C. WEAVER
OF WASHINGTON, D.C.

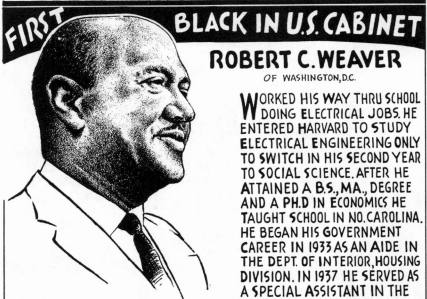

WORKED HIS WAY THRU SCHOOL DOING ELECTRICAL JOBS. HE ENTERED HARVARD TO STUDY ELECTRICAL ENGINEERING ONLY TO SWITCH IN HIS SECOND YEAR TO SOCIAL SCIENCE. AFTER HE ATTAINED A B.S., MA., DEGREE AND A PH.D IN ECONOMICS HE TAUGHT SCHOOL IN NO. CAROLINA. HE BEGAN HIS GOVERNMENT CAREER IN 1933 AS AN AIDE IN THE DEPT. OF INTERIOR, HOUSING DIVISION. IN 1937 HE SERVED AS A SPECIAL ASSISTANT IN THE FEDERAL HOUSING AUTHORITY.

WOW!

SOCIAL SCIENCE IS NOT SO SHOCKING!

SWITCHED FROM ELECTRICITY TO SOCIAL SCIENCES.

DURING WORLD WAR II HE WAS WITH, THE WAR MANPOWER COMM. LATER HE TAUGHT AT COLUMBIA U., AND N.Y.U. IN NEW YORK. IN 1956 HE BECAME DEPUTY STATE HOUSING COMMISSIONER FOR N.Y. HE SERVED AS BOARD CHAIRMAN IN THE NAACP. IN 1961 HE WAS APPOINTED HEAD OF THE FHA (HOUSING) BY PRES. KENNEDY. HE WROTE FOUR BOOKS. AWARDED THE 47th SPINGARN MEDAL (NAACP). PRES. JOHNSON NAMED HIM TO TO HIS CABINET IN 1966 – THE FIRST BLACK U.S. SECRETARY OF HOUSING. SINCE LEAVING GOVERNMENT HE HAS ENTERED IN THE FIELD OF EDUCATION IN-URBAN AFFAIRS.

WON THE 1962 SPINGARN MEDAL. (NAACP)

WROTE 4-BOOKS "THE NEGRO GHETTO"

NOT BAD

Geo LEE

© 1972 George L. Lee Feature Service

FIRST 50-YEARS in POLITICS

REP. AUGUSTUS F. HAWKINS

ELECTED TO THE U.S. CONGRESS IN '62 FROM THE 21st CONG. DIST., OF LOS ANGELES, CA. THE 5th BLACK TO JOIN DAWSON (ILL), POWELL (NY), DIGGS (MI) AND NIX (PA). IN 1984 HAWKINS REMAINS FIGHTIN' FOR MINORITIES. BORN IN SHREVEPORT, LA., IN 1907 YOUNGEST OF 5 CHILDREN. AT 10 HIS FAMILY MOVED TO LOS ANGELES. EARNED AN AB DEGREE IN ECONOMICS AT UCLA (1931). STUDIED BUSINESS AT USC's GRADUATE SCHOOL... BUT THE POVERTY SITUATION WAS SO BAD IN CALIFORNIA HE TURNED TO POLITICS AND CAMPAIGNED VIGOROUSLY FOR "FDR". RAN

Geo Lee

FOR THE CALIF. STATE ASSEMBLY AND ELECTED IN 1934. SERVED 28 YEARS. "GUS" FOUGHT FOR A CALIF. "FAIR EMPLOYMENT PRACTICES ACT" - PASSED 1959. AUTHORED MANY LAWS FOR THE POOR. A GREAT ASSEMBLY CAREER. HE WENT TO CAPITOL HILL WHERE TO-DAY (1984) HE IS CHAIRMAN OF THE HOUSE EMPLOYMENT OPPORTUNITIES SUBCOMMITTEE.

1984 Geo L. Lee Feature Service

BEST KNOWN FOR THE HUMPHREY-HAWKINS FULL EMPLOYMENT AND BALANCED GROWTH ACT... SIGNED INTO LAW - 1978. ON CAPITOL HILL, GUS IS A QUIET GIANT!

A QUIET GIANT

ONLY 5'5" HE CASTS A BIG SHADOW.

POLICE CHIEF FIRST

BOSTON DANIELS

WHO BECAME KANSAS CITY, KANSAS' FIRST BLACK POLICE CHIEF - WAS ONCE A PULLMAN PORTER!

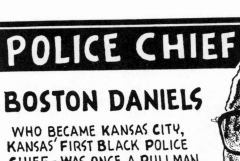

BORN IN FORMAN, ARK., THE SON OF A COTTON FARMER AND A PREACHER. HE STUDIED AGRICULTURE AND TAILORING AT ARKANSAS A&M FOR TWO YEARS. IN 1928 WENT TO KANSAS CITY TO SEEK HIS FORTUNE. FOR MANY YEARS HE WORKED ODD JOBS AND THEN BECAME A PULLMAN PORTER. ON FEB 1, 1945 HE WAS APPOINTED AS A PATROLMAN ON KANSAS CITY'S POLICE FORCE. FOR 25-YEARS HE FOUGHT CRIME

AND IN JULY 1970 MAYOR McDOWELL APPOINTED DANIELS POLICE CHIEF...FIRST BLACK OF A CITY WITH 170,000 POP. HE SOLVED THOUSANDS OF CRIMES DURING HIS CAREER AS JUST-A-COP. A REAL CRIMEBUSTER!

Geo Lee

LOUIS JORDAN
1909 – 1975

ONCE KNOWN AS THE "KING OF THE JUKE BOXES"...STAGE, SCREEN AND RADIO PERSONALITY WHO ROSE FROM PLAYING THE COCKTAIL LOUNGES TO THE BIGGEST THEATRES AND NIGHT CLUBS IN THE COUNTRY WITH HIS "TYMPANY FIVE" WAS TAUGHT MUSIC BY HIS FATHER, A MUSIC TEACHER. BORN IN BRINKLEY, ARK., HE GRADUATED FROM THE ARKANSAS BAPTIST COLLEGE. DURING THE 1940s, HE BECAME

STONE COLD DEAD IN THE MARKET

ROUTE 66

BEWARE!

A BIG NAME IN THE FIELD OF ENTERTAINMENT. A FINE MUSICIAN AND SHOWMAN HE ALSO WAS A COMPOSER. HIS RECORDINGS WERE TOP SELLERS. SINGING THE BLUES IN HIS STYLE WAS BIG. THO HIS BAND WAS SMALL HE RATED ALONG WITH HAMPTON AND CALLOWAY AS A BOX-OFFICE STAR. HIS BIG HITS WERE MANY – "BEWARE BROTHER BEWARE" – "CALDONIA" – "ON THE OUTSKIRTS OF TOWN" AND "KNOCK ME A KISS" – AMONG THEM.

FIRST BLACK EPISCOPAL BISHOP

BISHOP JOHN M. BURGESS

WAS ELECTED AMERICA'S FIRST BLACK BISHOP OF THE EPISCOPAL DIOCESE OF MASS. IN JAN 1970. HE BECAME LEADER OF 125,000 MEMBERS CONDUCTING SERVICES IN THE CHAPEL OF THE DIOCESAN HOUSE IN BOSTON. HE REACHED HIS POSITION AT THE AGE OF 61. A NATIVE OF GRAND RAPIDS, MICH., HE WORKED HIS WAY THRU COLLEGE WASHING DISHES IN A FRATERNITY HOUSE. BISHOP BURGESS RECEIVED HIS B.A. AND M.A. DEGREES IN SOCIOL-OGY AT THE U OF MICH. HIS RELIGIOUS STUDIES AT THE EPISCOPAL THEO-LOGICAL SCHOOL IN CAMBRIDGE,

MASS. THE SON OF A DINING CAR WAITER, HE WAS ORDAINED IN 1934. LATER SERVED IN OHIO, CHAPLAIN OF HOWARD U. AND CANON OF WASHINGTON CATHEDRAL. APPOINTED AN ARCHDEACON OF BOSTON (1956). ELECTED TO SUFFRAGAN (ASSISTING) BISHOP IN 1962.

GEO LEE

© 1975 George L. Lee Feature Service

SINGER · DANCER · ACTOR

1911
1984

IN BUBBLING BROWN SUGAR

Geo
LEE

AVON LONG

ONCE TURNED DOWN A THEOLOGI-CAL SEMINARY SCHOLARSHIP TO DANCE THE GOLDEN STAIRS OF SHOW BIZ. FAME WAS NO ACCIDENT, 3 PARTS HARD WORK...1 PART LUCK, IT LED TO SUCCESS. HE WON A SCHOLAR-SHIP TO BOSTON CONSERVATORY TO STUDY MUSIC AND ONE TO STUDY BALLET WITH RUSSIKOFF. BORN IN BALTIMORE, MD. HE LEFT HOME AT 15, GOING TO BOSTON.

PLAYED VAUDEVILLE AND NIGHT CLUBS. FIRST WON ATTENTION SINGING "BROWN BOY" AT HARLEM'S COTTON CLUB (1933). THEN ONE NIGHT ... HIS STAGE DEBUT IN A REVIVAL OF GERSHWIN'S "PORGY AND BESS," PLAYING "SPORTIN' LIFE" HIS SINGING - "IT AIN'T NECESSARILY SO"... STOPPED THE SHOW.' AN OVER-NIGHT SUCCESS (1938). HE APPEARED IN MANY BROADWAY MUSICALS ALSO

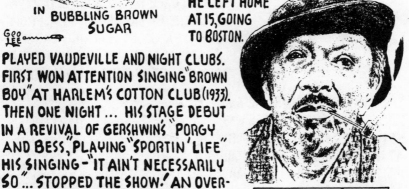

AS THE ELDERLY "CHICKEN GEORGE" IN ROOTS II

FILMS AND T.V. AT 73, WAS STILL PERFORMING IN "BUBBLING BROWN SUGAR" IN W. GER., ON N. YEARS EVE (1983) HIS LAST. DIED FEB 1984, (N.Y.)

1984 Geo L. Lee Feature Service

DISTINGUISHED EDUCATOR

DR. HUGH M. GLOSTER

PRESIDENT OF MOREHOUSE COLLEGE IN ATLANTA, GA., (1967) HAS HAD A VERY INTERESTING CAREER IN EDUCATION. BORN ON MAY 11, 1911 IN BROWNSVILLE, TENN. AFTER HIS EARLY SCHOOLING HE WENT TO LE MOYNE COLLEGE FOR HIS JUNIOR STUDIES. THEN TO MOREHOUSE COLLEGE WHERE HE BECAME EDITOR OF THE MAROON TIGER, THE STUDENT PUBLICATION. GRADUATED WITH HIGH HONORS AND A B.A. DEGREE IN 1931. A PHI BETA KAPPA STUDENT HE EARNED HIS M.A. FROM ATLANTA U. HIS TEACHING CAREER BEGAN AT LE MOYNE AND HE ROSE RAPIDLY TO PROFESSOR. IN 1941 JOINED

Geo
LEE

THE FACULTY OF MOREHOUSE AND SERVED BRILLIANTLY. IN FEB 1943 HE RECEIVED HIS PH.D IN ENGLISH AT NEW YORK UNIV., HE MAINTAINED A STRAIGHT "A" AND WAS REGARDED AS ONE OF THE MOST DISTINGUISHED STUDENTS IN THE GRADUATE SCHOOL. DURING WW II SERVED AS A USO PROGRAM DIRECTOR. LATER BECAME DEAN OF FACULTY AT HAMPTON INSTIT.

1980 GEO L. LEE FEATURE SERVICE

IN 1961-62 - VISITING PROFESSOR OF AMERICAN LITERATURE - WARSAW, POLAND

1960 DIRECTOR, EXPERIMENTAL COLLEGE FOR HAMPTON. VIRGIN. IS.

FULBRIGHT PROFESSOR OF ENGLISH AT HIROSHIMA U. IN JAPAN

1961-62 IN AMERICAN SPECIALISTS PROGRAM - AT UNIVERSITIES - CRACOW, POL. VALENCIA, SPAIN DAR ES SALAAM, TANGANYIKA

AS DEAN AT HAMPTON HE WENT TO SIERRA LEONE AS SUPV. OF AN AID PROGRAM.

IN 1969, RECEIVED A FORD GRANT TO THE ASIAN CONFERENCE - IN HONG KONG

MOREHOUSE COLLEGE FOUNDED - 1867

"THE COLLEGE OF PRESIDENTS" 14 COLLEGE HEADS FROM MOREHOUSE

KNOCK ON ANY DOOR!

WILLARD MOTLEY
1912 - 1965

WHO WROTE THE BEST SELLER - KNOCK ON ANY DOOR - WHICH WAS PUBLISHED IN 1947, SPENT 8 YEARS WRITING THE NOVEL. AFTER THE FIRST DRAFT IT HAD 600,000 WORDS. FOUR YEARS LATER IT HAD BEEN CUT TO 240,000 WORDS. HE WAS SIX YEARS WRITING HIS SECOND NOVEL - LET NO MAN WRITE MY EPITAPH. BOTH WERE MADE INTO MOVIES.

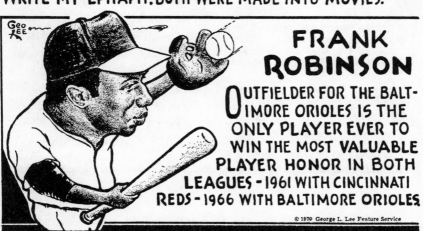

FRANK ROBINSON

OUTFIELDER FOR THE BALTIMORE ORIOLES IS THE ONLY PLAYER EVER TO WIN THE MOST VALUABLE PLAYER HONOR IN BOTH LEAGUES - 1961 WITH CINCINNATI REDS - 1966 WITH BALTIMORE ORIOLES

© 1970 George L. Lee Feature Service

71

HIS HONOR....

JUDGE GEORGE N. LEIGHTON

OF THE **U.S.** DISTRICT COURT NORTHERN DIST., OF ILL (1975). RESIDENT OF CHICAGO, HE WAS BORN IN NEW BEDFORD, MASS., OF NATIVE CAPE VERDE PARENTS (1912). HE LEFT SCHOOL IN THE 7th GRADE TO BECOME A MERCHANT SEAMAN ON AN OIL-TANKER. LEIGHTON WON A VERDEAN ESSAY CONTEST AND A $200 PRIZE AS INITIAL TUITION FOR COLLEGE. REJECTED BY HOWARD U., BECAUSE HE HAD NOT ATTENDED HI-SCHOOL, BUT HE WAS ACCEPTED AS AN "UNCLASSIFIED STUDENT." HE MADE THE

GEO LEE

DEAN'S HONOR ROLL THE FIRST YEAR (1936). GRADUATED HOWARD U, IN 1940. SERVED AS AN INFANTRY CAPTAIN IN WORLD WAR II. IN 1946

CAPE VERDE ISLANDS, AN ARCHIPELAGO BELONGING TO PORTUGAL; OFF THE WEST AFRICAN COAST, 14 ISLANDS IN THE GROUP. THE FIRST SETTLERS ON THE ISLANDS IMPORTED NEGRO SLAVES FROM THE AFRICAN COAST. THE PORTUGUESE GOVERNMENT FREED THE SLAVES 1854....

LISTEN

WHERE'S THE CAPE VERDE ISLANDS?

RECEIVED A LLB LAW DEGREE FROM HARVARD. ADMITTED TO THE MASS., BAR (1946). THE ILL., BAR IN 1947. THE U.S. SUPREME COURT BAR (1958). A DISTINGUISHED LAWYER FOR 18 YEARS. ELECTED A CIRCUIT COURT JUDGE OF COOK COUNTY (ILL) 1964. NAMED TO THE APPELLATE COURT OF ILL., 1969. A CAPE VERDEAN MAKING GOOD!

1978 GEO L. LEE FEATURE SERVICE

FIRST 3-STAR GENERAL

LT. GEN. BENJAMIN O. DAVIS JR.

FIRST BLACK AIR-FORCE GENERAL WAS BORN IN WASHINGTON D.C. HE STARTED HIS MILITARY CAREER AS A CADET AT WEST POINT, GRADUATING IN JUNE 1936.

Geo LEE

HE WON HIS WINGS AT THE TUSKEGEE ARMY AIR-FIELD IN 1942. DURING WORLD WAR II HE LED THE ALL-BLACK 99TH PURSUIT SQUADRON. WON THE DISTINGUISHED FLYING CROSS IN 1944. THE FIRST BLACK TO COMMAND A U.S. MILITARY BASE AT GODMAN FIELD, KY. HE HEADED THE 332ND FIGHTER BOMBER GROUP AND IN 1945 WON THE SILVER STAR. A BRILLIANT MILITARY MAN HE WAS PROMOTED TO BRIG. GENERAL IN 1954; MAJOR GEN., IN 1959 AND LT. GEN., IN 1967. WHEN HE RETIRED IN 1970 HE WAS DEPUTY CHIEF, U.S. STRIKE COMMAND AND RECEIVED THE PRESIDENTIAL CITATION AND DISTINGUISHED SERVICE MEDAL. TRULY A LEADER!

1980 GEO L. LEE FEATURE SERVICE

FIRST BLACK PRES. OF PAINE

1915
1974

DR. LUCIUS H. PITTS

DURING THE FALL OF 1971 HE BECAME THE FIRST BLACK PRESIDENT OF PAINE COLLEGE IN AUGUSTA, GA., IN ITS 89-YEAR HISTORY. THE BRILLIANT GEORGIAN EDUCATOR GRADUATED FROM PAINE IN 1941. HE RECEIVED 2 MASTERS DEGREES—FISK U. AND ATLANTA U. HIS FIRST JOB WAS AT MILES COLLEGE IN BIRMINGHAM, ALA... A SCHOOL THAT SPECIALIZES IN TEACHER EDUCATION. HE WAS A PART-TIME TEACHER AND DIRECTOR OF YOUTH WORK. PITTS SERVED WITH A CHURCH GROUP IN AUGUSTA BEFORE HIS PRINCIPALSHIP OF HALSEY-COBB

Geo LEE

INSTITUTE IN CORDELE, GA. FOR 5-YEARS WAS EXEC. SECRETARY OF THE GEORGIA TEACHERS AND EDUCATION ASSN (1955-60). IN 1961 RETURNED TO MILES AS ITS PRESIDENT AND PERFORMED MIRACLES PUTTING MILES ON A SOUND BASIS. HE PERSUADED DR. MUNRO A DEAN AT HARVARD TO RESIGN AND COME TO MILES' FRESHMEN'S AID.

MILES COLLEGE A PRIVATE SCHOOL

FOLLOW ME

ACADEMIC ACCREDITATION IN 1969

SUCCESS

INCREASED ITS BUDGET

DOUBLED ITS ENROLLMENT

UNDER DR. PITTS LEADERSHIP MILES GAINED NATIONAL NOTICE.

1977, George L. Lee Feature Service

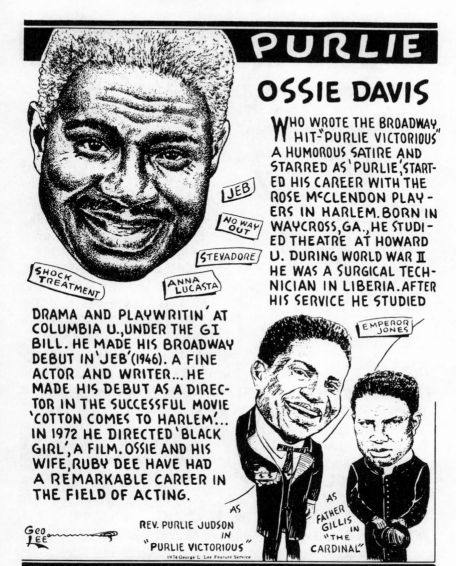

PURLIE

OSSIE DAVIS

WHO WROTE THE BROADWAY HIT "PURLIE VICTORIOUS" A HUMOROUS SATIRE AND STARRED AS 'PURLIE', STARTED HIS CAREER WITH THE ROSE McCLENDON PLAYERS IN HARLEM. BORN IN WAYCROSS, GA., HE STUDIED THEATRE AT HOWARD U. DURING WORLD WAR II HE WAS A SURGICAL TECHNICIAN IN LIBERIA. AFTER HIS SERVICE HE STUDIED DRAMA AND PLAYWRITIN' AT COLUMBIA U., UNDER THE GI BILL. HE MADE HIS BROADWAY DEBUT IN 'JEB' (1946). A FINE ACTOR AND WRITER... HE MADE HIS DEBUT AS A DIRECTOR IN THE SUCCESSFUL MOVIE 'COTTON COMES TO HARLEM'... IN 1972 HE DIRECTED 'BLACK GIRL', A FILM. OSSIE AND HIS WIFE, RUBY DEE HAVE HAD A REMARKABLE CAREER IN THE FIELD OF ACTING.

JEB

NO WAY OUT

STEVADORE

SHOCK TREATMENT

ANNA LUCASTA

EMPEROR JONES

Geo Lee

AS REV. PURLIE JUDSON IN "PURLIE VICTORIOUS"

1974 George L. Lee Feature Service

AS FATHER GILLIS IN "THE CARDINAL"

CLASSIC COMPOSER

ULYSSES KAY

DISTINGUISHED PROFESSOR OF MUSIC AT LEHMAN COLLEGE OF THE CITY UNIV. OF N.Y. BORN IN TUCSON, ARIZ., IN 1917. HIS UNCLE JOE OLIVER THE IMMORTAL.... "JAZZ CORNETIST" URGED HIM TO PLAY THE PIANO. HE BEGAN HIS MUSICAL STUDIES AT UNIV. OF ARIZONA AND EARNED A SCHOLARSHIP TO THE EASTMAN SCHOOL OF MUSIC AND RECEIVED A MASTERS DEGREE. ALSO STUDIED UNDER SUCH TEACHERS AS OTTO LUENING AT COLUMBIA, PAUL HINDEMITH AT YALE. IN 1947 HE COMPOSED "SUITE FOR STRINGS" AND "CONCERTO FOR ORCHESTRA" (1948). KAY WON THE PRIX DE ROME AWARD AND A FULBRIGHT FELLOWSHIP. WENT TO ITALY TO STUDY (1949-52). IN 1965 STARTED TEACHING CAREER AT BOSTON UNIV., AT U.C.L.A IN 1966-67. PROFESSOR OF MUSIC AT LEHMAN COLLEGE IN 1968. FIRST BLACK TO CONDUCT THE PHILA. ORCHESTRA IN HIS OWN WORK "CHARIOTS," AT SARATOGA FESTIVAL (1979).

THAT'S IT

UMBRIAN SCENE 1963

SONG OF JEREMIA 1947

PHOEBUS ARISE 1959

THE BOOR 1955

JUBILEE 1976

FANTASY VARIATIONS 1964

QUINTET CONCERTO 1974

(A FEW OF HIS MANY CREDITS)

1980 GEO L. LEE FEATURE SERVICE

PIONEER of MODERN JAZZ

THELONIOUS MONK

ONE OF THE GREAT JAZZ PIANIST-COMPOSERS AND FOUNDING FATHERS OF THE MODERN JAZZ REVOLUTION. A NATIVE OF NEW YORK'S SAN JUAN HILL SECTION. PLAYED THE ORGAN AT 12, IN THE FIRST BAPTIST CHURCH. A 14-YEAR OLD STUDENT AT STUYVESANT HI, HE WOULD LEAVE SCHOOL AND PLAY AT HARLEM HOUSE-RENT PARTIES. HE STARTED HIS CAREER IN THE MID-THIRTIES WHEN HE WON AN AMATEUR CONTEST AT THE FAMED APOLLO THEATER AND A RETURN ENGAGEMENT AT $10-A-SHOW. MONK WON SO MANY TIMES, THE MANAGER HAD TO BAR HIM. AT 17 PLAYED WITH A BAND FOR A TRAVEL-ING DIVINE HEALER. AT 18, IN KELLY'S STABLE BAR ON 52nd St. WHILE PLAYING AT MINTON'S PLAYHOUSE MONK BE-GAN TO WRITE DOWN HIS MUSIC. THE ADVANCED STYLE SO IMPRESSED THE OTHER MUSICIANS THAT HIS INFLUENCE SPREAD. ALONG WITH PARKER AND GILLESPIE, THE THREE WERE THE MOST RESPONSIBLE FOR THE GREAT CHANGE IN MODERN AMERICAN MUSIC. THRU THE YEARS HIS SUCCESS HAS BEEN HIGHLIGHTED WITH HIS QUARTET AND RECORDINGS.

1978 Geo L.Lee Feature Service

COMMISSIONER of EDUCATION

DR. WILSON C. RILES

FIRST BLACK TO BE ELECTED CALIFORNIA'S SUPERINTEN- DENT OF PUBLIC INSTRUCTION OF 5-MILLION PUPILS (1970).... ONCE TAUGHT IN A SMALL ELEMENTARY SCHOOL ON AN APACHE INDIAN RESERVATION AT PISTOL CREEK, ARIZ. BORN NEAR ALEXANDRIA, LA., IN 1917. ORPHANED AT 11, HE WORKED HIS WAY THROUGH ARIZ. STATE COLLEGE. SERVED 3-YEARS IN THE ARMY AIR-FORCE. RETURN- ED TO ARIZ. STATE AND EARNED HIS MASTER'S DEGREE. ENTERED THE TEACHING FIELD AND SOON

Geo LEE

WINNER OF NAACP'S 1973 SPINGARN MEDAL -THE 58th MEDALIST. "THE HIGHEST OR NOBLEST ACHIEVEMENT BY AN AMERICAN BLACK DUR- ING THE PRECEDING YEAR OR YEARS." DR. RILES SERVES AS A REGENT OF U. OF CALIF.

ROSE TO ASSOCIATE SUPT. OF THE CAL- IF. STATE DEPT OF EDUCATION IN 1965. PROMOTED TO DEPUTY SUPT., IN 1969. ACCEPTED THE CHALLENGE OF SEEK- ING THE ELECTED OFFICE OF COMM- ISSIONER OF EDUCATION AND WON WITH OVER 3-MILLION VOTES. A BIG MAN, 6 FOOT 6 IN A BIG JOB!

1980 GEO L. LEE FEATURE SERVICE

HE SINGS THE BLUES ♩

JOE WILLIAMS

LEGENDARY BLUES SINGER WHO ADDED SOPHISTICATION AND EMERGED A SINGER OF SOUL, POP AND JAZZ. BORN IN CORDELE, GA., IN 1918. RAISED IN CHICAGO FROM AGE 2. HIS MOTHER SANG IN A CHURCH CHOIR AND INFLUENCED HIS MUSICAL CAREER. AT 17 HE SOUGHT A CHANCE WITH JOHNNY LONG'S BAND FOR NO PAY...LATER $5-A NIGHT. IN THE 1940s SANG WITH MANY GROUPS...HAWKINS, TATE, KIRK, HAMPTON. IN 1950 MET COUNT BASIE IN CHICAGO AND SANG FOR 10-WEEKS. IN 1954, MET BASIE

Geo LEE

A FEW OF HIS HITS "ALRIGHT, OK, YOU WIN" "TEACH ME TONIGHT" "SMACK DAB IN THE MIDDLE" "I AIN'T GOT NOTHING BUT THE BLUES" "GOING TO CHICAGO"

WON DOWNBEAT'S POLL 5-TIMES AS BEST BLUES SINGER.

1984 GEO L. LEE FEATURE SERVICE

AGAIN IN N.Y...THIS TIME JOE BECAME A MEMBER OF THE BAND. THEY RECORDED A SMASH HIT IN 1955..."EVERY DAY I HAVE THE BLUES"...JOE SKYROCKETED TO NATIONAL FAME. IN 1961 HE LEFT BASIE AND WENT ON TOUR. OVER THE YEARS HIS DISTINCTIVE STYLE...BETTER THAN EVER!

79

FIRST LADY of SONG

ELLA FITZGERALD

WHO HAILS FROM NEWPORT NEWS, VA., STARTED HER CAREER AS A TEENAGER SINGING IN AMATEUR CONTESTS AT THE APOLLO THEATER AND THE HARLEM OPERA HOUSE IN NEW YORK CITY. SHE AUDITIONED FOR THE LATE CHICK WEBB WHO DIDN'T LIKE THE IDEA OF A GIRL SINGER FOR HIS BAND. HE GAVE HER A TRIAL WHEN HE PLAYED AN ENGAGEMENT AT YALE U. IT WAS NO PAY FOR ELLA BUT IF SHE WENT OVER, THE JOB WAS HERS. THE REST IS HISTORY. IN 1938, ELLA AND CHICK RECORDED HER OWN SONG, "A TISKET A-TASKET," AND SHE SKYROCKETED TO FAME AND FORTUNE. ONE OF THE TRULY GREAT VOCALISTS OF OUR TIME. IN 1968 SHE WAS AWARDED NEW YORK'S FIRST CULTURAL AWARD AN HONOR-FOR EXCEPTIONAL ACHIEVEMENT IN THE PERFORMING OR CREATIVE ARTS. A GREAT ARTIST WHO CONTINUES TO BE THE NO. 1 - FEMALE SINGER IN THE WORLD.

© 1971 George L. Lee Feature Service

SEN. EDWARD W. BROOKE
OF MASS.

FIRST NEGRO **U.S.**SENATOR SINCE RECONSTRUCTION. ELECTED FROM MASS(GOP) IN 1966. BORN IN WASH D.C.-HE GRADUATED FROM HOWARD U. IN 1941 AS A PRE-MED BUT SWITCHED TO LAW. WON BRONZE STAR AS AN INFANTRY CAPT. IN ITALY IN WORLD WAR II. EARNED LAW DEGREE AT BOSTON U.-IN 1961 HE WAS APPOINTED CHAIRMAN OF THE BOSTON FINANCE COMM. IN 1962 HE WAS ELECTED ATTY-GEN.OF MASS.

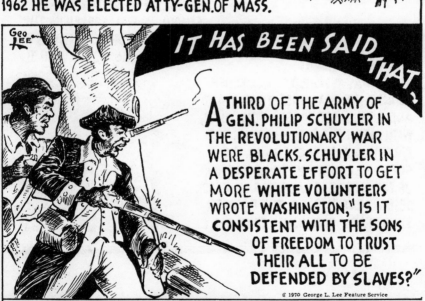

IT HAS BEEN SAID THAT,

A THIRD OF THE ARMY OF GEN. PHILIP SCHUYLER IN THE REVOLUTIONARY WAR WERE BLACKS. SCHUYLER IN A DESPERATE EFFORT TO GET MORE **WHITE VOLUNTEERS** WROTE WASHINGTON," IS IT CONSISTENT WITH THE SONS OF FREEDOM TO TRUST THEIR ALL TO BE DEFENDED BY SLAVES?"

© 1970 George L. Lee Feature Service

81

A PHILADELPHIA LAWYER

WHO BECAME THE FIRST BLACK U.S. SECRETARY OF TRANSPORTATION

WILLIAM T. COLEMAN JR

BRILLIANT LAWYER SERVED IN THE FORD ADMINISTRATION CABINET. A REPUBLICAN WITH A DISTINGUISHED CAREER IN PUBLIC SERVICE...SWORN INTO OFFICE ON MAR 7,1975. A NATIVE OF PHILADELPHIA AND A GRADUATE OF U.OF PENNA., WITH AN A.B. SUMMA CUM LAUDE DEGREE IN POLITICAL SCIENCE. ENTERED HARVARD LAW SCHOOL IN 1941. SERVED IN THE ARMY AIR CORPS WINNING HIS WINGS DURING WORLD WAR II.

IN 1943 WAS ASSIGNED AS A DEFENSE COUNSEL. HE RETURNED TO HARVARD AND GRADUATED MAGNA CUM LAUDE, WITH AN L.L.B. DEGREE IN 1946. THE FIRST BLACK LAW CLERK IN U.S. SUPREME COURT HISTORY. CO-AUTHOR OF THE NAACP LEGAL BRIEF ON SCHOOL DESEGREGATION (1954). THE FORMER SECRETARY CONTINUES TO EXCEL.
(1978)

ONE OF HIS CHIEF PROBLEMS WHILE SEC'Y OF TRANSPORTATION WAS THE LANDING OF THE SUPERSONIC JET-CONCORDE ON U.S. SOIL. FINALLY HE OK'D A 16-MONTH TRIAL BASIS. (MAR 1976)

RACHEL

JACKIE

RACHEL ROBINSON

MET JACKIE ROBINSON AT **UCLA**. THEY MARRIED IN 1946 AND SPENT THEIR HONEYMOON AT MONTREAL'S BASEBALL SPRING-TRAINING CAMP IN DAYTONA BEACH, FLA. DURING HER LIFE WITH BASEBALL'S FIRST BLACK 'HALL OF FAMER'... SHE HAD A CAREER OF **PSYCHIATRIC NURSING**. A SUPERVISOR AT THE ALBERT EINSTEIN COLLEGE OF MEDICINE IN 1963... LATER AN ASSOCIATE PROFESSOR OF CLINICAL PSYCHIATRY AT THE YALE SCHOOL OF MEDICINE. SINCE THE DEATH OF JACKIE IN OCT., 1972... SHE CHANGED HER CAREER TO BUSINESS AND BECAME HEAD OF THE JACKIE ROBINSON DEVELOPMENT CORP... BUILDING LOW AND MIDDLE INCOME HOUSING UNITS-YONKERS, BROOKLYN AND MANHATTAN. RACHEL FOUNDED THE JACKIE ROBINSON MANAGEMENT IN 1973 AS THE AGENT FOR THE $50-MILLION DOLLARS IN HOUSING UNITS. QUITE AN ACCOMPLISHMENT... HATS OFF TO RACHEL!

OVER 1,100 DWELLING UNITS

FROM NURSING TO CONSTRUCTION.

84

BUSINESSMAN · AUTHOR

DEMPSEY J. TRAVIS

HIGHLY SUCCESSFUL CHICAGO REALTOR AND PRESIDENT OF SIVART MORTGAGE CORP., THE LARGEST BLACK MORTGAGE BANKERS IN AMERICA. BY HARD WORK AND DILIGENCE HE ROSE FROM POVERTY TO MILLIONAIRE. BORN IN CHICAGO ON FEB 25, 1920. A DU SABLE HI GRADUATE (1939). HIS BIG INTEREST IN SCHOOL WAS PIANO AND JAZZ MUSIC. HE HAD HIS OWN ORCHESTRA AT 15. DURING WORLD WAR II HE JOINED THE ARMY (1942-46). ENTERED WILSON JUNIOR COLLEGE AND FINISHED THE 24-MONTH

COURSE IN 16-MONTHS. WENT TO ROOSEVELT U., AND STUDIED REAL ESTATE. AFTER GRADUATION (1949) HE OPENED HIS FIRST REALTY OFFICE THEN, TRAVIS INS., AGENCY ('50). IN 1953 THE SIVART MORTGAGE CORP. GRADUATED FROM NORTHWESTERN U., SCHOOL OF MORTGAGE BANKING ('69). HIS ACHIEVEMENTS ARE MANY. LISTED IN WHO'S WHO IN AMERICA!

DEMPSEY TURNED AUTHOR. HE WROTE A BOOK..."AN AUTOBIOGRAPHY OF BLACK CHICAGO"...THE LIFE AND TIMES OF BLACK CHICAGO. HE PUBLISHED IT HIMSELF AND IT MADE THE BEST SELLER LIST. HIS NEXT BOOK ON...JAZZ.

1983 Geo L. Lee Feature Service

85

HIS HONOR THE MAYOR

WALTER E. WASHINGTON
OF WASH. D.C.

FIRST "MAYOR" OF THE NATION'S CAPITAL, APPOINTED BY PRESIDENT JOHNSON ON SEPT 21,1967. THE FIRST BLACK TO HEAD A MAJOR U.S. CITY. BORN IN DAWSON, GA., AND REARED IN JAMESTOWN, N.Y. EDUCATED AT HOWARD UNIVERSITY. AN AUTHORITY ON HOUSING. HE STARTED HIS CAREER IN HOUSING IN 1941. HE WAS CHAIRMAN OF THE N.Y. CITY HOUSING AUTHORITY AT $35,000 A-YEAR WHEN HE ACCEPTED $28,500 AS MAYOR. POSITION NOW— $40,000. RE-APPOINTED BY PRES. NIXON.

25-YEARS AGO
JAMES A. "BILLBOARD" JACKSON
OF INDIANAPOLIS, IND.

WAS A NOTED BUSINESS PUBLICIST AND SPECIAL REPRESENTATIVE OF THE STANDARD OIL CO., OF NEW JERSEY. A TOP MARKET RESEARCHER HE WAS CHIEF OF THE SMALL BUSINESS SECTION OF THE U.S. DEPT., OF COMMERCE (1927-1933). DURING THE FIRST WORLD WAR HE SERVED IN THE MILITARY INTELLIGENCE BUREAU, GENERAL STAFF. HE ACQUIRED HIS NICKNAME "BILLBOARD" WHEN HE WAS ON THE STAFF OF THE BILLBOARD MAGAZINE.

© 1973 George L. Lee Feature Service

TID·BITS

RUBY I. BELL

FIRST BLACK WOMAN TO BE EMPLOYED AS AN OBSERVER IN METEOROLOGY FOR THE UNITED STATES WEATHER BUREAU IN ATLANTIC CITY, N.J., IN 1944. A NATIVE OF BROOKLYN, N.Y., AND A GRADUATE OF HUNTER COLLEGE (1943).

FIRST

HOW'S THE WEATHER?

EASY

'SATCHEL' PAIGE

WHILE PITCHING FOR THE PITTSBURGH CRAWFORDS IN THE NEGRO NAT'L LEAGUE IN 1933....... WON 31-GAMES... 21-IN *SUCCESSION!*

WENDELL P. DABNEY

BUTTERFLY McQUEEN

COMEDIENNE STAR OF RADIO, STAGE AND MOVIES

AT THE AGE OF 80-YEARS IN 1946 HE OWNED, EDITED AND MANAGED THE "ONE-MAN" PAPER THE CINCINNATI UNION" AMERICA'S MOST UNUSUAL PAPER. MR. DABNEY WAS ONCE ONE OF THE COUNTRY'S FINEST BANJO AND GUITAR PLAYERS. HE WAS PAY-MASTER OF CINCINNATI FOR 25 YEARS.

WITH HER NATURAL FLUTTERY VOICE. IN 1939 SHE PLAYED "PRISSY"-A-13 YEAR OLD GIRL IN THE TOP PICTURE - "GONE WITH THE WIND"-ALTHO SHE WAS 29-YEARS OLD.

Geo LEE

© 1973 George L. Lee Feature Service

A LIFETIME JUDGE

JUDGE DAMON J. KEITH

HIGHLY RESPECTED JUDGE OF THE U.S. COURT OF APPEALS, SIXTH CIRCUIT (MICH). A FEDERAL JUDGE APPOINTED BY PRES. L.B. JOHNSON IN 1967. BORN IN DETROIT ON JULY 4, 1922. DURING THE DEPRESSION HIS FAMILY WAS ON WELFARE BUT THEY PUT HIM THROUGH NORTHWESTERN HIGH SCHOOL. HE WORKED HIS WAY THROUGH WEST VIRGINIA STATE U., A BLACK COLLEGE, EARNING HIS DEGREE. AFTER 3-YEARS IN THE U.S. ARMY,

Geo LEE

HE ENTERED THE HOWARD U. LAW SCHOOL IN 1946. HE RETURNED TO DETROIT AND AFTER ODD JOBS, SET-UP A LAW PRACTICE...BECAME INTERESTED IN POLITICS AND CIVIL RIGHTS. IN 1963 WAS ONE OF 6 LAWYERS FROM DETROIT TO DISCUSS CIVIL RIGHTS WITH PRES. J.F.K. IN 1964 WAS NAMED AS CHAIRMAN OF MICHIGAN CIVIL RIGHTS COMM. HE IS A COMMISSIONER OF THE STATE BAR (MICH). HONORARY DOCTOR OF LAW DEGREE FROM YALE UNIV (1981).

HIS AWARDS ARE MANY - SINCE 1974 HE HAS BEEN NAMED AMONG THE 100 MOST INFLUENTIAL BLACK AMERICANS BY EBONY MAGAZINE.

RECIPIENT OF NAACP'S COVETED 1974 SPINGARN MEDAL AS THE OUTSTANDING BLACK AMERICAN.

1983 Geo L. Lee Feature Service

HEADS ROMAN CATHOLIC DIOCESE

BISHOP JOSEPH L. HOWZE

IN MARCH, 1977 HE BECAME THE FIRST BLACK TO HEAD A CATHOLIC DIOCESE IN THE U.S., THE NEWLY CREATED DIOCESE OF BILOXI, MISS. BORN IN DAPHNE, ALA., AUG 30, 1923. HIS EARLY EDUCATION IN DAPHNE AND MOBILE. GRADUATED FROM ALABAMA STATE U., 1948. HIS CAREER STARTED AS A TEACHER OF BIOLOGY AND CHEMISTRY. HE JOINED THE CATHOLIC CHURCH... SOON HE DECIDED TO ENTER THE PRIESTHOOD. HE WAS ACCEPTED

HIS BILOXI DIOCESE HAS:
92-PRIESTS
106-SISTERS
64-BROTHERS
42-PARISHES
17-ELEMENTARY SCHOOLS
6-HI-SCHOOLS
51,000 CATHOLICS.

BY THE RALEIGH, N.C., DIOCESE. HOWZE STUDIED AT BUFFALO DIOCESAN PREPARATORY SEMINARY (N.Y.), CHRIST KING SEMINARY AND ST. BONAVENTURE U. (N.Y.). ON MAY 7, 1959 WAS ORDAINED A PRIEST. NAMED AS AUXILIARY BISHOP OF NATCHEZ-JACKSON DIOCESE IN 1972 BY THE POPE... THE 2nd U.S. BLACK TO BECOME A ROMAN CATHOLIC BISHOP.'

1984 Geo L. Lee Feature Service

A STAR IS BORN

RUBY DEE

THE BRILLIANT ACTRESS OF RADIO, SCREEN, STAGE AND TV WAS BORN IN CLEVELAND, OHIO. EDUCATED IN NYC, SHE RECEIVED HER B.A. FROM HUNTER COLLEGE. HER FIRST ACTING ROLE WAS IN THE AMERICAN NEGRO THEATRE PRODUCTION-ON STRIVERS ROW. HER FIRST PROFESSIONAL ROLE WAS A BIT PART IN "SOUTH PACIFIC" STARRING CANADA LEE IN 1942. IN

FIRST BLACK RADIO SOAP OPERA ACTRESS TO STAR ON A NAT'L NETWORK SHOW (1955). - WHEN SHE WAS CAST IN A NON-BLACK ROLE IN - "THIS IS NORA DRAKE"

RUBY WAS A BIG HIT AS "LUTIEBELLE" IN THE BROADWAY COMEDY- "PURLIE VICTORIOUS" IN 1961.

1946 SHE STARRED IN ANNA LUCASTA ON BROADWAY. MARRIED OSSIE DAVIS IN 1948. WENT TO HOLLYWOOD IN 1950 AND PLAYED SIDNEY POITIER'S SISTER IN- "NO WAY OUT" AND APPEARED WITH HIM IN-"GO MAN GO"-"EDGE OF THE CITY"-THE VIRGIN ISLANDS AND THE BIG HIT"-"A RAISIN IN THE SUN." PLAYED SHAKES-PEARE ROLE IN - KING LEAR WITH (1965) MORRIS CARNOVSKY WHO ONCE TAUGHT HER ACTING. IN 1971 HAD A ROLE IN THE MOVIE-TO BE YOUNG, GIFTED AND BLACK. THE MOTHER OF 3-CHILDREN AND AN ACTRESS OF RARE ABILITY!

Geo Lee

© 1977 George L. Lee Feature Service

AGGRESSIVE EDITOR...

CHARLES B. ARMSTRONG SR

NEWSPAPER PUBLISHER AND EDITOR OF THE CHICAGO METRO NEWS WHOSE REPUTATION HAS BEEN GAINED BY ITS COMMUNITY AFFAIRS INVOLVEMENT. KNOWN AS A FIGHTER IN BLACK PRESS CIRCLES FOR HIS COURAGE AND DEDICATION FOR THE TRUTH. BORN IN NASHVILLE, TENN., IN 1923. HE RECEIVED HIS EARLY EDUCATION IN NASHVILLE AND COLUMBIA, TENN AND GRADUATED FROM CHICAGO'S PARKER HIGH. SERVED 3-YEARS IN THE U.S. ARMY DURING WORLD WAR II. IN 1946 HE ENTERED FISK UNIV., MAJORING IN HISTORY AND GRADUATED WITH HONORS

Geo LEE

(1950). HE TOOK GRADUATE STUDIES IN EDUCATION AT CHICAGO'S DE PAUL UNIV., AND TAUGHT HISTORY IN THE PUBLIC SCHOOLS. ENTERED POLITICS AS A PRECINCT CAPTAIN AND PRES., OF THE 4TH WARD YOUNG REPUBLICANS (1961-62). RAN FOR ALDERMAN IN 1963. SEEKING TO SPEAK-OUT HE JOINED THE CHICAGO COURIER STAFF.

1984 Geo L. Lee Feature Service

IN 1965 HE STARTED HIS OWN PAPER THE CHICAGO SOUTH SUBURBAN NEWS. UNDER HIS STRONG AGGRESSIVE LEADERSHIP IT GREW INTO THE CHICAGO METRO NEWS-FIGHTING FOR TRUTH AND EQUALITY FOR ALL PEOPLE.'

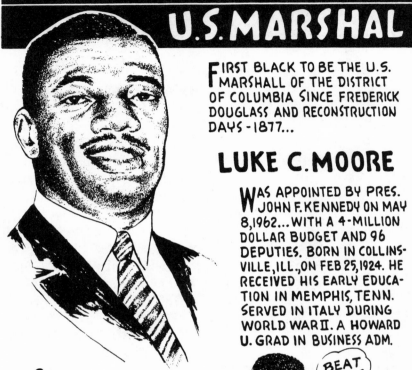

U.S. MARSHAL

FIRST BLACK TO BE THE U.S. MARSHALL OF THE DISTRICT OF COLUMBIA SINCE FREDERICK DOUGLASS AND RECONSTRUCTION DAYS - 1877...

LUKE C. MOORE

WAS APPOINTED BY PRES. JOHN F. KENNEDY ON MAY 8, 1962... WITH A 4-MILLION DOLLAR BUDGET AND 96 DEPUTIES. BORN IN COLLINSVILLE, ILL., ON FEB 25, 1924. HE RECEIVED HIS EARLY EDUCATION IN MEMPHIS, TENN. SERVED IN ITALY DURING WORLD WAR II. A HOWARD U. GRAD IN BUSINESS ADM.

GEO LEE

EARNED HIS LAW DEGREE FROM GEORGETOWN U... HE HAD A KEY ROLE IN THE JAMES MEREDITH, U. OF MISS., CASE. LUKE WAS ASSIGNED TO PROTECT THE MOBSTER KILLER, VALACHI... FROM THE WASH, D.C. JAIL TO NEW YORK AND BACK... TO TESTIFY AT THE GRAND JURY. VALACHI HAD A $100,000 BOUNTY ON HIS HEAD!

BEAT IT!

WHERE'S VALACHI

MARSHAL LUKE

I WANT VALACHI

FEDERAL RESERVE BOARD GOVERNOR

EMMETT J. RICE

NOTED ECONOMIST IS THE SECOND BLACK TO SIT ON THE POWERFUL BOARD WHICH OVERSEES THE NATIONS ECONOMIC POLICY (JUN 1979). PREVIOUSLY, SENIOR V.P. OF THE NAT'L BANK OF WASHINGTON (D.C.). BORN IN FLORENCE, S.C., EARNED HIS B.A. AND M.A. DEGREES AT CITY COLLEGE (N.Y.). SERVED IN THE U.S. AIR-FORCE. EARNED HIS PH.D. IN ECONOMICS AT U. OF CALIF (BERK.) IN 1955. TAUGHT AT CORNELL U. JOINED THE FEDERAL RESERVE SYSTEM (1960). WORKED FOR THE TREAS. DEPT. PRES. JOHNSON NAMED DR. RICE AN ALTERNATE-DIRECTOR FOR THE U.S. WORLD BANK (1966). A FULBRIGHT FELLOW!

SECRET SERVICE AGENT

CHARLES L. GITTENS

SPECIAL AGENT IN-CHARGE OF VITAL OPERATIONS IN THE DISTRICT OF COLUMBIA (1971). THE FIRST BLACK SECRET SERVICE AGENT (1956) A NATIVE OF CAMBRIDGE, MASS. AFTER HIGH SCHOOL HE JOINED THE ARMY AS A TROMBONE PLAYER IN THE BAND. EARNED A COMMISSION... GAVE IT UP AND WENT BACK TO SCHOOL... NO. CAROLINA COLLEGE, GRADUATED 1955. PASSED SECRET SERVICE EXAM. RETIRED - 1979.

Geo LEE

1980 GEO L. LEE FEATURE SERVICE

MEDGAR EVERS
1925 - 1963

BORN AND EDUCATED IN MISS. HE GRADUATED FROM ALCORN COLLEGE. AS FIELD SECRETARY OF THE NAACP HE FOUGHT FOR THE CIVIL RIGHTS OF HIS PEOPLE. DURING WORLD WAR II. HE SERVED IN THE ARMED FORCES AND SURVIVED THE NORMANDY INVASION - FIGHTING FOR DEMOCRACY - ONLY TO LOSE HIS LIFE AT HOME - FIGHTING FOR HIS RIGHTS!

ERROLL GARNER
OF PITTSBURGH, PA.

ONE OF THE GREATEST JAZZ PIANISTS WHOSE PIANO PERFECTION AND COMPOSITIONS HAVE WON EVERY JAZZ AWARD IN MUSICAL HISTORY - CAN'T READ A NOTE OF MUSIC - HIS MUSIC IS RECORDED THEN WRITTEN.

1921–1977

© 1970 George L. Lee Feature Service

GENERAL COUNSEL AT G.M.

OTIS M. SMITH

HEADS THE PRESTIGIOUS LEGAL STAFF OF GENERAL MOTORS, THE WORLD'S SECOND LARGEST INDUSTRIAL CORP. TO EXXON. APPOINTED TO THE TOP SPOT IN 1977. BORN IN MEMPHIS, HE GRADUATED FROM HIGH SCHOOL WITH A COLLEGE SCHOLARSHIP. ..BUT DIDN'T HAVE THE MONEY TO PAY FOR HIS MEALS. SO HE GOT A $60-A-MONTH JOB AT THE TENNESEE STATE CAPITOL IN NASHVILLE AS A MESSENGER AND PORTER. HE SAVED ENOUGH TO ENTER FISK U., AND WAS WORKING HIS WAY WHEN WORLD WAR II STEPPED IN AND HE HAD

TO QUIT SCHOOL. SERVED 3-YEARS IN THE ARMY AIR-FORCE'S 447th BOMB GROUP UNTIL 1946. GOT HIS FIRST GM JOB AS A NICKEL BUFFER. HE WENT BACK TO SCHOOL. EARNED HIS LAW DEGREE FROM THE CATHOLIC U., (WASH,D.C.) IN 1950. WENT INTO PRIVATE PRACTICE WITH ATTY. DUDLEY MALLORY AND A BRILLIANT LAW CAREER!

CHAIRMAN MICHIGAN PUBLIC COMMISSION

FIRST BLACK ELECTED STATE AUDITOR GENERAL — MICHIGAN 1961

MICHIGAN SUPREME COURT - 6 YEARS 1966

GM's LEGAL DEPT- 1967

ASS'T GEN COUNSEL 1975

VICE- PRES. 1975

GENERAL COUNSEL - 1977

1981 GEO L. LEE FEATURE SERVICE

FIRST BLACK ASSOC. PRESS SEC'Y.

ANDREW HATCHER

A TOP NEWSMAN AND PUBLIC RELATIONS EXPERT WHO AIDED PIERRE SALINGER IN THE CAMPAIGN THAT ELECTED JOHN F. KENNEDY TO THE PRESIDENCY IN 1960. PRES. KENNEDY APPOINTED HATCHER AS THE FIRST BLACK ASSOCIATE PRESS SECRETARY IN 1961 ALONG WITH PRESS SEC'Y SALINGER. A NATIVE OF PRINCETON, N. J., HE WAS A GRADUATE OF SPRINGFIELD COLLEGE (MASS). IN 1948 HE BECAME MANAGING EDITOR OF THE SAN FRANCISCO SUN-REPORTER A BLACK NEWSPAPER. LATER ANDREW TEAMED WITH SALINGER AND THEY HANDLED

MANY POLITICAL CAMPAIGNS. IN 1959 HE WAS ASS'T INDUSTRIAL COMMISSIONER OF CALIFORNIA. AFTER THE KENNEDY ASSASSINATION HE CONTINUED WITH PRES. JOHNSON UNTIL 1964. MR. HATCHER JOINED THE HILL AND KNOWLTON, INC., PUBLIC RELATIONS FIRM IN 1967 AS VICE-PRES. AND SENIOR VICE-PRESIDENT IN 1971.

© 1986 George L. Lee Feature Service

PRINCE OF DARKNESS

MILES DAVIS III

"JAZZ MUSICIAN OF THE YEAR" DOWN BEAT'S 1981 WINNER.

Geo LEE

A JAZZ TRUMPETER LEGEND IN HIS OWN TIME. HIS STYLE AND LEADER-SHIP HAS LEFT ITS IMPRINT IN THE JAZZ WORLD OF MUSIC. AFTER 5-YEARS ABSENCE HE RETURNED IN 1981 AT THE KOOL JAZZ FESTIVAL. BORN IN 1926 IN ALTON, ILL., AND RAISED IN EAST ST. LOUIS, ILL. HIS FATHER A DENTIST WHO RAISED PRIZE HOGS AS A HOBBY, HIS MOTHER A MUSIC TEACHER. MILES PLAYED TRUMPET IN HIGH SCHOOL. AFTER GRADUATION HE WENT TO N.Y. CITY, STUDIED AT JUILLIARD SCHOOL OF MUSIC. IN 1945 JOINED CHARLIE PARKER'S BAND PLAYING THE NIGHT CLUB CIRCUIT. IN 1948 LEFT PARKER...FORMED HIS OWN GROUP...RECORDED "BIRTH OF THE COOL". A NEW JAZZ ERA BEGAN. TOURED ENGLAND IN CONCERT IN 1960. SUCCESS WAS RISING. HIS ALBUM IN 1969..."BITCHES BREW", A BIG SELLER! HE EMERGED A GIANT. A MASTER FROM BEBOP TO COOL AND COOL TO PROGRESSIVE HIS NOTORIOUSLY RECLUSIVE NATURE MADE HIM THE "PRINCE OF DARKNESS."

HIS "THE MAN WITH THE HORN" VOTED "JAZZ ALBUM OF THE YEAR" 1981

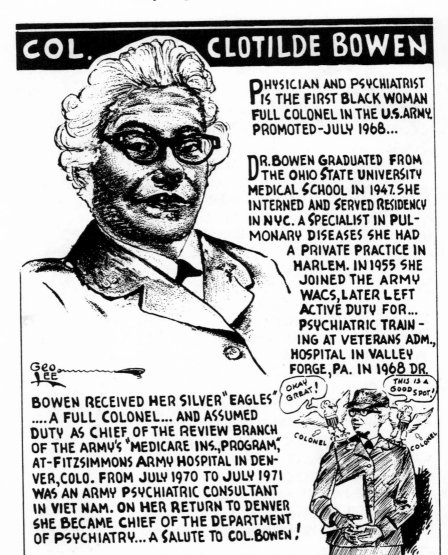

COL. CLOTILDE BOWEN

PHYSICIAN AND PSYCHIATRIST IS THE FIRST BLACK WOMAN FULL COLONEL IN THE U.S. ARMY. PROMOTED-JULY 1968...

DR. BOWEN GRADUATED FROM THE OHIO STATE UNIVERSITY MEDICAL SCHOOL IN 1947. SHE INTERNED AND SERVED RESIDENCY IN NYC. A SPECIALIST IN PULMONARY DISEASES SHE HAD A PRIVATE PRACTICE IN HARLEM. IN 1955 SHE JOINED THE ARMY WACS, LATER LEFT ACTIVE DUTY FOR... PSYCHIATRIC TRAINING AT VETERANS ADM., HOSPITAL IN VALLEY FORGE, PA. IN 1968 DR.

Geo LEE

BOWEN RECEIVED HER SILVER "EAGLES" ....A FULL COLONEL... AND ASSUMED DUTY AS CHIEF OF THE REVIEW BRANCH OF THE ARMY'S "MEDICARE INS., PROGRAM", AT-FITZSIMMONS ARMY HOSPITAL IN DENVER, COLO. FROM JULY 1970 TO JULY 1971 WAS AN ARMY PSYCHIATRIC CONSULTANT IN VIET NAM. ON HER RETURN TO DENVER SHE BECAME CHIEF OF THE DEPARTMENT OF PSYCHIATRY... A SALUTE TO COL. BOWEN!

© 1977. George L. Lee Feature Service

98

UP THE POLITICAL LADDER

CARL B. STOKES
OF CLEVELAND, OHIO

ONCE A LIQUOR ENFORCEMENT AGENT WHO BECAME THE FIRST BLACK MAYOR OF A BIG CITY–CLEVELAND. A HIGH SCHOOL DROP-OUT WHO JOINED THE ARMY DURING WORLD WAR II. AFTER HIS DUTY HE WENT BACK TO HIGH SCHOOL AND GRADUATED AT 21. LATER TO THE UNIV. OF MINNESOTA AND EARNED HIS B.S. DEGREE. HE TOOK LAW AT CLEVELAND'S -MARSHALL LAW SCHOOL. WITH A LAW DEGREE HE BECAME AN ASS'T CITY PROSECUTOR.

IN 1962 HE WAS ELECTED AS THE FIRST BLACK TO THE OHIO STATE LEGISLATOR. WITH A BACKGROUND OF EXPERIENCE HE RAN FOR MAYOR OF CLEVELAND IN 1965 AND LOST BY A VERY SLIM MARGIN. HIS NEXT EFFORT IN 1967 WAS SUCCESS-FUL. AFTER A 2-YEAR TERM HE WAS RE-ELECTED, ANOTHER FIRST. IN 1971 HE RECEIVED THE NATIONAL NEWSPAPER PUBLISHERS HIGHEST AWARD – THE RUSSWURM AWARD. PRIVATE CITIZEN STOKES IN 1972 LOOKS AHEAD TO NEW HORIZONS!

© 1972 George L. Lee Feature Service

and all that JAZZ

JOHN COLTRANE

ONE OF THE MOST INFLUENTIAL MUSICIANS OF HIS TIME AND CONSIDERED A GIANT IN CONTEMPORARY JAZZ. KNOWN BY FRIENDS AS "TRANE" HE WAS BORN IN HAMLET, N.C. THE SON OF A TAILOR WHO PLAYED MUSIC AS A HOBBY. "TRANE" STARTED MUSIC IN HISCHOOL IN PHILA, PA. LATER STUDIED AT

IN 1965 'TRANE' SWEPT THE ANNUAL DOWNBEAT READER'S POLL · TOP TENOR SAXOPHONIST · JAZZMAN OF THE YEAR · ELECTED TO HALL OF FAME · HIS "A LOVE SUPREME", RECORD OF THE YEAR!

ONLY 40 WHEN HE DIED IN 1967.

GEO LEE

THE ORNSTEIN SCHOOL OF MUSIC. PLAYED IN A U.S. NAVY BAND IN HAWAII. RETURNED TO THE STATES IN 1947. PLAYED WITH DIZZY AND SMALL GROUPS. FIRST REAL BREAK IN 1955 WITH THE MILES DAVIS QUINTET. HIS POPULARITY GREW.... IN 1960 FORMED HIS OWN QUARTET AND CREATED A STYLE IN MUSIC. HIS SOPRANO SAXOPHONE INTERPRETATION OF "MY FAVORITE THINGS" WON HIM ACCLAIM.

1979 GEO L. LEE FEATURE SERVICE

100

LEVI JACKSON

FIRST BLACK FOOTBALL PLAYER IN THE 245-YEAR HISTORY OF YALE UNIVERSITY IN 1946. ALSO THE FIRST BLACK TO BE ELECTED TEAM CAPTAIN IN 1949. HIS FATHER WAS DINING-HALL STEWARD AND WAITER AT YALE FOR 30 YEARS.

JUSTICE
FRANCIS E. RIVERS

FIRST BLACK ELECTED AS JUSTICE OF THE NEW YORK CITY COURT IN 1944 FOR A 10-YEAR TERM AT AN ANNUAL SALARY OF $17,500. A BRILLIANT YALE STUDENT HE WON HIS PHI BETA KAPPA KEY IN 1915... WORKED HIS WAY THRU BY WAITING TABLE - WASHING DISHES - COLLECTING BILLS.

KENNETH SPENCER

WHO SANG THE FAMED ROLE OF "JOE" IN THE SPECTACULAR PRODUCTION "SHOW BOAT" IN 1945 WAS THE FIRST SINGER EVER TO RECEIVE A ROSENWALD FELLOWSHIP. SPENCER ONCE UNDERSTUDIED FOR PAUL ROBESON IN "JOHN HENRY." HE WON AN EASTMAN SCHOOL OF MUSIC SCHOLARSHIP (ROCHESTER) AND GRADUATED IN 1938. KILLED IN A PLANE CRASH. (1964)

Geo. Lee

THE FIRST BLACK WOMAN TO BE APPOINTED IN THE U.S. DEPT. OF AGRICULTURE IN 1945 - ASSIGNED TO THE PATHOLOGICAL DIV. OF THE BUREAU OF ANIMAL INDUSTRY. A BACTERIOLOGIST SHE RECEIVED HER TRAINING AT HOUSTON COLLEGE AND THE UNIV. OF MICHIGAN.

CARRA DELL OWENS

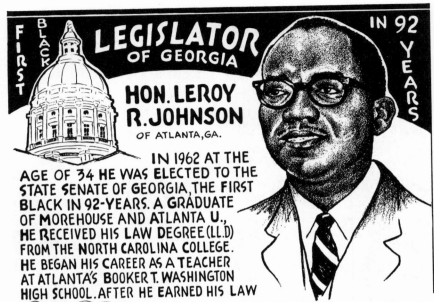

FIRST BLACK **LEGISLATOR** OF GEORGIA IN 92 YEARS

HON. LEROY R. JOHNSON
OF ATLANTA, GA.

IN 1962 AT THE AGE OF 34 HE WAS ELECTED TO THE STATE SENATE OF GEORGIA, THE FIRST BLACK IN 92-YEARS. A GRADUATE OF MOREHOUSE AND ATLANTA U., HE RECEIVED HIS LAW DEGREE (LL.D) FROM THE NORTH CAROLINA COLLEGE. HE BEGAN HIS CAREER AS A TEACHER AT ATLANTA'S BOOKER T. WASHINGTON HIGH SCHOOL. AFTER HE EARNED HIS LAW

DEGREE, HE BECAME THE FIRST BLACK CRIMINAL INVESTIGATOR IN THE DEEP SOUTH. WHEN NEW SENATORIAL DISTRICTS OPENED UP IN ATLANTA HE ENTERED INTO POLITICS AND WON IN THE 38TH DISTRICT. 1969 HE WAS APPOINTED CHAIRMAN OF THE SCIENTIFIC RESEARCH COMMITTEE, THE FIRST BLACK TO HEAD A STANDING COMMITTEE IN MODERN HISTORY. IN 1971 HE WAS HONORED BY THE BOYS' CLUB WORKERS WHEN HE WAS AWARDED THE HERMAN S. PRESCOTT AWARD. SEN. JOHNSON FIGHTS FOR CIVIL RIGHTS!

DISTINGUISHED JUDGE

A. LEON HIGGINBOTHAM

U.S. CIRCUIT JUDGE FOR THE THIRD CIRCUIT OF THE U.S. COURT OF APPEALS (PA) SINCE 1977. ONE OF AMERICA'S 10-OUTSTANDING YOUNG MEN OF 1963, NAMED BY THE U.S. JUNIOR CHAMBER OF COMMERCE. A NATIVE OF TRENTON, N.J., HE RECEIVED HIS B.A. FROM ANTIOCH COLLEGE AND HIS L.L.B. FROM YALE LAW SCHOOL. PRES. KENNEDY NOMINATED HIM FOR THE FEDERAL TRADE COMM., AND BECAME THE YOUNGEST MAN EVER APPOINTED TO THAT BODY(34). THE FIRST BLACK COMMISSIONER OF A FEDERAL REGULATORY AGENCY;

GEO LEE

AN ASS'T DISTRICT ATTORNEY IN PHILADELPHIA AND PRIVATE PRACTICE. IN 1964 WAS NOMINATED TO SERVE AS U.S. DIST. JUDGE FOR EASTERN DISTRICT OF PA., UNTIL 1977. HIGHLY RECEIVED BY THE AMERICAN BAR ASSOC.,"EXCEPTIONALLY WELL-QUALIFIED" BY UNANIMOUS VOTE.

1979 GEO L. LEE FEATURE SERVICE

THE JUDGE SPENT 10-YEARS WRITING "THE MATTER OF COLOR." A BOOK ON HOW THE LAW WAS USED TO KEEP INJUSTICE AND ASSURE SLAVERY DURING THE COLONIAL PERIOD.

HONORARY DEGREES

103

A TOP EDUCATOR

DR. MANFORD BYRD JR

A FINE EDUCATOR WITH LEADERSHIP QUALITIES WHO ROSE FROM CLASS-ROOM TEACHER TO DEPUTY SUPT., IN THE CHICAGO SCHOOLS IN 14-YEARS. BORN ON MAY 29, 1928 IN BREWTON, ALA., WHERE HE RECEIVED HIS EARLY EDUCATION. ON A SCHOLARSHIP HE ENTERED CENTRAL COLLEGE (IOWA), GRADUATING IN 1949 WITH A B.A. DEGREE. HE BEGAN TEACHING IN QUINCY, ILL... RECEIVED A M.A. FROM ATLANTA U., IN EDUCATIONAL PSYCH-OLOGY (1954) AND JOINED CHICAGO'S SCHOOL SYSTEM. STARTED IN HOW-LAND ELEM. BECAME ASS'T PRINCIPAL ('60). IN 1962, PRINCIPAL OF GOETH-ALS GUIDANCE CENTER. PRINCIPAL

Geo LEE

MANFORD BYRD FOR PRESIDENT!

IN JUNE, 1982 ELECT-ED PRESIDENT OF THE JOINT NEGRO APP-EAL, A NON-PROFIT CHARITABLE OR-GANIZATION. FIRST BLACK ASS'T MOD-ERATOR OF UNITED CHURCH OF CHRIST SYNOD IN 1971.

OF ENGLEWOOD HI ('65)... HIS FINE PROGRAMS, PRAISED BY PARENTS AND NOTED BY SUPT. REDMOND WHO REALIZED HIS POTENTIAL... MADE BYRD HIS ASS'ISTANT IN 1967. BYRD WAS NAMED DEPUTY SUP'T., OF INSTRUCTIONAL SERVICES (1968). THE HIGHEST RANK FOR A BLACK!

1984 Geo L. Lee Feature Service

104

HIS HONOR THE MAYOR

ERNEST N. MORIAL

WHO WON A SECOND TERM AS MAYOR OF NEW ORLEANS IN MARCH 1982, WAS THE FIRST BLACK MAYOR ELECTED IN 1977. A NATIVE OF NEW ORLEANS, HE GRADUATED FROM XAVIER UNIVERSITY IN 1951. THE FIRST BLACK GRADUATE OF LOUISIANA STATE UNIVERSITY LAW SCHOOL IN 1954. IN 1967 HE BECAME THE FIRST BLACK IN THE STATE LEGISLATURE IN THE 20th CENTURY. HE WAS SWORN IN AS A JUDGE OF THE ORLEANS PARISH (COUNTY) JUVENILE COURT IN 1971. LATER

Geo Lee

TWO DAYS AFTER HIS INAUGURATION IN 1978, NEW ORLEANS HAD 50-MILLION FLOOD DAMAGE. TWO MONTHS LATER ...GARBAGE WORKERS WENT ON.... STRIKE! MORIAL SHOWED HIS ABILITY AND LAID HIS FOUNDATION.

AN APPEALS COURT JUDGE. MAYOR MORIAL IS A PAST PRESIDENT OF ALPHA PHI ALPHA FRATERNITY. AN ORGANIZER AND FORMER DIRECTOR, BANK +TRUST CO. AND A TULANE UNIV. BOARD MEMBER. EXPERIENCE ...WILL AID HIS SECOND TERM.

1982 GEO L. LEE FEATURE SERVICE

Mayor Ernest N. Dutch Morial was elected Mayor of the City of New Orleans in 1978, and served for two terms until 1986. He served on the NAACP National Board of Directors from 1981 until his untimely death, December 24, 1989.

FROM-HOLMES COUNTY, MISS.

ROBERT G. CLARK

ON JAN 2,1968 HE WAS SWORN IN AS A MEMBER OF THE MISSISSIPPI LEGISLATURE... THE FIRST BLACK ELECTED TO THE STATE HOUSE OF REPRESENTATIVES IN 74-YEARS...FROM HOLMES COUNTY.' BORN IN EBENEZER,MISS., A SMALL TOWN IN RURAL HOLMES COUNTY, THE 5th-POOREST COUNTY IN THE NATION.EDUCATED AT JACKSON COLLEGE, HE BEGAN TEACHING AT HUMPHREY CTY. TRAINING SCHOOL. TO ADVANCE HIMSELF HE STUDIED FOR HIS MASTER'S DEGREE AT

IF BILBO'S STATUE COULD HAVE SPOKEN ~

GIT OUT BOY!

Geo LEE

HI!

MISSISSIPPI LEGISLATURE

CLARK

BILBO

MICHIGAN STATE AND PH.D AT THE U.OF MICH. HIGHLY EDUCATED HE STILL HAD TO BE TEACHER AND COACH. LATER HE BECAME DIRECTOR OF AN ANTI-POVERTY PROGRAM IN HIS COUNTY. IN 1967 HE TURNED TO POLITICS AND RAN AS AN INDEPENDENT FOR LEGISLATOR AND...WON!' AT AGE 38.

© 1976 George L. Lee Feature Service

$54.600.

DR. MARTIN LUTHER KING JR
1929-1968

THE BRILLIANT LEADER, WHO ADVOCATED NON-VIOLENCE, WON THE 1964 NOBEL PEACE PRIZE. AT THE AGE OF 35, HE BECAME THE YOUNGEST PERSON EVER, TO WIN THE COVETED HONOR. ALFRED NOBEL, WEALTHY FOUNDER OF THE PEACE PRIZE-WAS THE INVENTOR OF DYNAMITE.

CONGRESSWOMAN SHIRLEY CHISOLM
OF BROOKLYN, N.Y.

BECAME THE FIRST BLACK WOMAN IN U.S. HISTORY WHEN SHE WAS ELECTED TO THE 91st CONGRESS IN 1968. SHE STARTED HER RISE IN POLITICS, WHEN ELECTED TO THE N.Y. STATE ASSEMBLY. HOLDS A MASTERS DEGREE IN EDUCATION. SPEAKS FLUENT SPANISH.

GEO LEE

FIRST BLACK NAVAL CAPTAIN

CAPT. THOMAS D. PARHAM JR

CHIEF OF PASTORAL CARE SERVICE, OF THE CHAPLAIN CORPS WAS THE FIRST BLACK TO ATTAIN THE RANK OF CAPTAIN (MAR 1968) SINCE THE CIVIL WAR. BORN IN NEWPORT NEWS, VA. RECEIVED HIS HIGHER EDUCATION AT NORTH CAROLINA COLLEGE (DURHAM) EARNING A B.A. DEGREE. A B.A. AND M.A. IN THEOLOGY AT WESTERN THEOLOGICAL SEMINARY, PITTSBURGH, PA. AN ORDAINED PRESBYTERIAN MINISTER JOINED THE NAVY AS A CHAPLAIN (44).

SPECIAL ASS'T TO THE CHIEF OF NAVAL PERSONNEL FOR THE SCIENCE OF HUMAN RELATIONS (1968-70). ATTENDED THE AMERICAN U. IN WASH, D.C. FOR A PH.D IN SOCIOLOGY. HE SET UP HUMAN AFFAIRS COUNCILS AT VARIOUS NAVY BASES THROUGHOUT THE WORLD. CAPT. PARHAM IMPLEMENTED THE DEPT OF DEFENSE HUMAN GOALS PROGRAM. HIS PASTORAL EFFORTS HAVE BEEN INSPIRING!

1990 140 L. LEE FEATURE SERVICE

AWARDED THE MERITORIOUS SERVICE MEDAL IN 1970....

WELL DONE

"FOR HIS UNIQUE CONTRIBUTION TO THE PROMOTION OF HUMAN RELATIONS WITHIN THE NAVY DURING A PERIOD OF GREAT SOCIAL CHANGE."

A SUPERSTAR

RAYMOND St. JACQUES

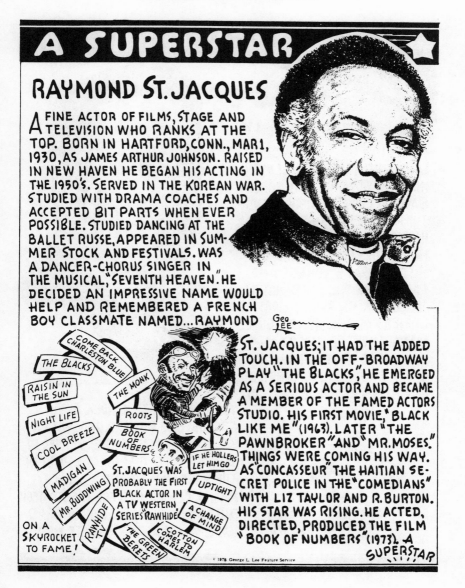

A FINE ACTOR OF FILMS, STAGE AND TELEVISION WHO RANKS AT THE TOP. BORN IN HARTFORD, CONN., MAR 1, 1930, AS JAMES ARTHUR JOHNSON. RAISED IN NEW HAVEN HE BEGAN HIS ACTING IN THE 1950's. SERVED IN THE KOREAN WAR. STUDIED WITH DRAMA COACHES AND ACCEPTED BIT PARTS WHEN EVER POSSIBLE. STUDIED DANCING AT THE BALLET RUSSE, APPEARED IN SUMMER STOCK AND FESTIVALS. WAS A DANCER-CHORUS SINGER IN THE MUSICAL, "SEVENTH HEAVEN." HE DECIDED AN IMPRESSIVE NAME WOULD HELP AND REMEMBERED A FRENCH BOY CLASSMATE NAMED... RAYMOND

Geo LEE

COME BACK CHARLESTON BLUE

THE BLACKS

THE MONK

RAISIN IN THE SUN

NIGHT LIFE

Roots

COOL BREEZE

BOOK OF NUMBERS

IF HE HOLLERS LET HIM GO

MADIGAN

St. JACQUES WAS PROBABLY THE FIRST BLACK ACTOR IN A TV WESTERN SERIES "RAWHIDE"

UPTIGHT

MR. BUDDWING

A CHANGE OF MIND

RAWHIDE TV

THE GREEN BERETS

COTTON COMES TO HARLEM

ON A SKYROCKET TO FAME!

© 1978 George L. Lee Feature Service

St. JACQUES; IT HAD THE ADDED TOUCH. IN THE OFF-BROADWAY PLAY "THE BLACKS," HE EMERGED AS A SERIOUS ACTOR AND BECAME A MEMBER OF THE FAMED ACTORS STUDIO. HIS FIRST MOVIE, "BLACK LIKE ME" (1963). LATER "THE PAWNBROKER" AND "MR. MOSES." THINGS WERE COMING HIS WAY. AS "CONCASSEUR" THE HAITIAN SECRET POLICE IN THE "COMEDIANS" WITH LIZ TAYLOR AND R. BURTON. HIS STAR WAS RISING. HE ACTED, DIRECTED, PRODUCED THE FILM "BOOK OF NUMBERS" (1973). A **SUPERSTAR**

SPACE DIRECTOR

ISAAC T. GILLAM IV

DIRECTOR OF THE DRYDEN FLIGHT RESEARCH CENTER (NASA) AT EDWARDS AIR-FORCE BASE IN CALIF., (JUN 18, 1978) AND THE HIGHEST RANKING BLACK IN THE NASA PROGRAM. UNDER HIS COORDINATED EFFORTS THE HISTORIC SAFE VOYAGE AND LANDING OF THE SPACE SHUTTLE "COLUMBIA" ON APRIL 14, 1981. JOINED NASA (1963) AS A RESOURCE MANAGEMENT SPECIALIST...HIS BRILLIANCE IN THE FIELD OF SPACE ENGINEERING CARRIED HIM TO HIS ENVIABLE POSITION!

GEO LEE

HAIL COLUMBIA

GILLAM EARNED NASA'S HIGHEST AWARD THE DISTINGUISHED SERVICE MEDAL.

A NATIVE OF LITTLE ROCK, ARK... A GRADUATE OF HOWARD UNIV., WITH A B.S. IN MATHEMATICS (1952). SERVED IN THE AIR-FORCE (1953-63) AS A PILOT IN THE KOREAN WAR AND A LAUNCH MISSILE COMMANDER FOR THE STRATEGIC AIR COMMAND. ALSO STUDIED GRADUATE WORK AT TENN. STATE UNIV.

1981 GEO L. LEE FEATURE SERVICE

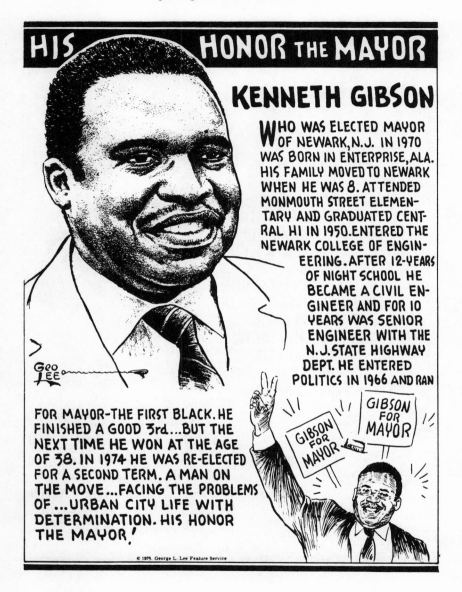

HIS HONOR THE MAYOR

KENNETH GIBSON

WHO WAS ELECTED MAYOR OF NEWARK, N.J. IN 1970 WAS BORN IN ENTERPRISE, ALA. HIS FAMILY MOVED TO NEWARK WHEN HE WAS 8. ATTENDED MONMOUTH STREET ELEMENTARY AND GRADUATED CENTRAL HI IN 1950. ENTERED THE NEWARK COLLEGE OF ENGINEERING. AFTER 12-YEARS OF NIGHT SCHOOL HE BECAME A CIVIL ENGINEER AND FOR 10 YEARS WAS SENIOR ENGINEER WITH THE N.J. STATE HIGHWAY DEPT. HE ENTERED POLITICS IN 1966 AND RAN FOR MAYOR-THE FIRST BLACK. HE FINISHED A GOOD 3rd...BUT THE NEXT TIME HE WON AT THE AGE OF 38. IN 1974 HE WAS RE-ELECTED FOR A SECOND TERM. A MAN ON THE MOVE...FACING THE PROBLEMS OF...URBAN CITY LIFE WITH DETERMINATION. HIS HONOR THE MAYOR!

GIBSON FOR MAYOR

GIBSON FOR MAYOR

111

PILOT · WEATHERMAN · MUSICIAN

JIM TILMON

CHICAGO'S WMAQ-TV CHANNEL 5 (NBC) WEATHER FORECASTER SINCE 1974. AN AMERICAN AIR-LINES CO-PILOT CAPTAIN FLYING 727's. HE RELAXES BY PLAYING FIRST CLARINET WITH THE HIGH-LAND PARK SYMPHONY ORCHESTRA. BORN IN GUTHRIE, OKLA., HIS MOTHER A TEACHER AND HIS FATHER A HIGH SCHOOL PRINCIPAL. GRADUATE OF LINCOLN UNIV, (MO) WITH A MUSIC DEGREE (1955). JOINED THE ARMY FLIGHT SCHOOL AND PILOTED LIGHT AIRCRAFT AND HELI-COPTERS IN GERMANY. HE LEFT THE ARMY AS A CAPTAIN. IN 1965 STARTED AS A FLIGHT ENGINEER WITH THE AMERICAN AIRLINES. MADE HIS

GEO LEE

SUNNY
SUNNY STORMS
T-STORMS

CHICAGO'S FIRST BLACK MAN TO DO THE WEATHER....

TV DEBUT AS HOST ON A WEEKLY TALK SHOW "OUR PEOPLE" A BLACK AWARENESS FORMAT ON WTTW (1968). LATER HOSTED AND PRODUCED.... "TILMON TEMPO" A COMMENTARY, CULTURAL, ENTERTAINMENT SHOW ON WMAQ-TV. A VERY BUSY MAN IN THE AIR AND ON THE AIR.'

1981 GEO L. LEE FEATURE SERVICE

ACTOR·COMEDIAN

1933
1976

GODFREY CAMBRIDGE

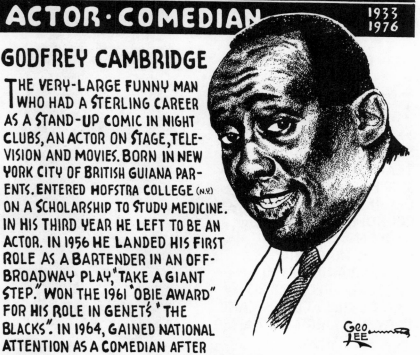

THE VERY-LARGE FUNNY MAN WHO HAD A STERLING CAREER AS A STAND-UP COMIC IN NIGHT CLUBS, AN ACTOR ON STAGE, TELEVISION AND MOVIES. BORN IN NEW YORK CITY OF BRITISH GUIANA PARENTS. ENTERED HOFSTRA COLLEGE (N.Y.) ON A SCHOLARSHIP TO STUDY MEDICINE. IN HIS THIRD YEAR HE LEFT TO BE AN ACTOR. IN 1956 HE LANDED HIS FIRST ROLE AS A BARTENDER IN AN OFF-BROADWAY PLAY, "TAKE A GIANT STEP." WON THE 1961 "OBIE AWARD" FOR HIS ROLE IN GENET'S "THE BLACKS". IN 1964, GAINED NATIONAL ATTENTION AS A COMEDIAN AFTER

Geo
LEE

PURLIE VICTORIOUS
TIME FOR LAUGHTER
THE BISCUIT EATER
NATURE'S WAY
IN- "COME BACK CHARLESTON BLUE"
THE PRESIDENT'S ANALYST
COTTON COMES TO HARLEM
IN- "WATERMELON MAN" PLAYED WITH WHITEFACE MAKE-UP!
A FEW OF HIS MANY CREDITS......

HIS APPEARANCES ON JACK PAAR'S, "TONIGHT SHOW." APPEARED ON BROADWAY, IN MOVIES AND TELEVISION. HIS ACTING CAREER WAS GOING GREAT WHEN HE WAS CUT DOWN BY A HEART ATTACK AT THE AGE OF 43, WHILE PLAYING ROLE OF IDI AMIN IN TV'S "VICTORY AT ENTEBBE." GODFREY LECTURED IN 1973 ON THE ABUSE OF DRUGS.

1979 GEO L. LEE FEATURE SERVICE

MAYOR RICHARD G. **HATCHER**
OF GARY, IND.

THE FIRST **BLACK** MAYOR OF GARY, WAS THE **FASTEST SPRINTER** ON HIS HOMETOWN, MICHIGAN CITY HIGH SCHOOL TEAM. ON A TRACK SCHOLARSHIP HE EARNED A **B.A.** DEGREE IN GOV'T AND ECONOMICS FROM **INDIANA U.**, WHERE HE RAN TRACK, HIGH JUMPED AND PLAYED FOOTBALL. RECEIVED HIS LAW DEGREE AT VALPARAISO U., BY WORKING AS A WAITER IN A HOSPITAL.

Geo Lee

BISHOP RICHARD ALLEN
OF AFRICAN METHODIST EPISCOPAL CHURCH (PHILA. PA)

1760 1831

IN NOV. 1787, THE **NEGRO** MEMBERS OF THE **METHODIST** SOCIETY OF PHILADELPHIA, DUE TO PREJUDICE LEFT AND ORGANIZED THE **BETHEL SOCIETY.** IN 1794 RICHARD ALLEN A LEADING PREACHER FOUNDED THE **FIRST** BETHEL A.M.E. CHURCH IN THE **U.S.** HE BECAME THEIR **FIRST** BISHOP (1816).

FORD FOUNDATION HEAD

FRANKLIN A. THOMAS

Geo
LEE

FIRST BLACK PRESIDENT OF THE FORD FOUNDATION, AMERICA'S RICHEST PHIL-ANTHROPIC AGENCY. AFTER A YEAR-LONG SEARCH AND 300 CANDIDATES HE WAS CHOSEN IT'S 7th PRESIDENT (JUNE 1979). BORN AND REARED IN BROOKLYN'S BED-FORD-STUYVESANT NEIGHBORHOOD ON MAY 27, 1934. HIS FATHER DIED WHEN HE WAS 12. A STAR IN HI-SCHOOL BASKET-BALL. THE 6'4" WORKED HIS WAY THROUGH COLUMBIA COLLEGE. BASKET-BALL TEAM CAPTAIN AND MADE THE ALL-IVY TEAM. GRADUATED IN 1956. SERVED 4-YEARS IN THE STRATEGIC AIR-COMMAND AS A NAVIGATOR FLY-ING REFUELING MISSIONS OVER THE

ARCTIC CIRCLE. GRADUATED FROM THE COLUMBIA LAW SCHOOL WITH MOOT COURT HONORS (1963). AN ASS'T U.S. ATTORNEY (1964); DEPUTY POLICE COMR., FOR LEGAL MATTERS. IN 1967 ROBT F. KENNEDY NAMED HIM TO HEAD THE NEW BEDFORD-STUYVES-ANT RESTORATION CORP. IN 10-YEARS

- FORD FOUNDATION WANTED A PRESIDENT. $120,000 SALARY

THANKS; BUT I NEED A CHALLENGE

MR. THOMAS TURNED DOWN JIMMY CARTER'S JOB OFFER...BUT GLADLY ACCEPTED THE FORD FOUNDATION!

I'D LIKE TO MAKE YOU SECRETARY OF HUD MR. THOMAS ....

A SUCCESSFUL URBAN RENEWAL. IN 1977 WENT INTO PRIVATE LAW PRACTICE.

1980 GEO L. LEE FEATURE SERVICE

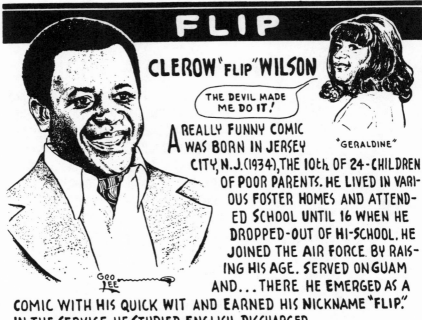

FLIP

CLEROW "FLIP" WILSON

THE DEVIL MADE ME DO IT!

"GERALDINE"

A REALLY FUNNY COMIC WAS BORN IN JERSEY CITY, N.J. (1934), THE 10th OF 24-CHILDREN OF POOR PARENTS. HE LIVED IN VARIOUS FOSTER HOMES AND ATTENDED SCHOOL UNTIL 16 WHEN HE DROPPED-OUT OF HI-SCHOOL. HE JOINED THE AIR FORCE. BY RAISING HIS AGE. SERVED ON GUAM AND...THERE HE EMERGED AS A COMIC WITH HIS QUICK WIT AND EARNED HIS NICKNAME "FLIP." IN THE SERVICE HE STUDIED ENGLISH. DISCHARGED IN 1954 HE TOOK A JOB AS A BELL-HOP IN A SAN FRANCISCO HOTEL. FLIP KEPT PEOPLE LAUGHING AND DECIDED ON A CAREER AS A COMIC. HE SET A 15-YEAR GOAL TO SUCCEED. WRITING HIS OWN MATERIAL HE APPEARED IN SMALL CLUBS. IN 1965 REDD FOXX GOT HIM A SPOT ON THE "TONIGHT SHOW", IT WAS INSTANT "SUCCESS". IN 1970 HE HAD HIS OWN SHOW, "THE FLIP WILSON SHOW." FLIP CREATED...GERALDINE, REV. LEROY, FREDDIE THE PLAYBOY, SONNY THE WHITEHOUSE JANITOR.

1979 GEO L. LEE FEATURE SERVICE

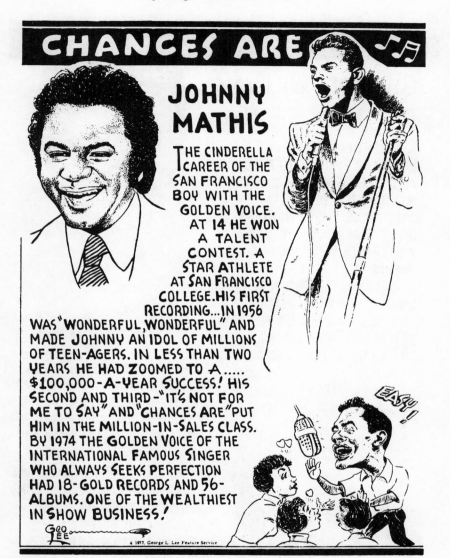

CHANCES ARE

JOHNNY MATHIS

THE CINDERELLA CAREER OF THE SAN FRANCISCO BOY WITH THE GOLDEN VOICE. AT 14 HE WON A TALENT CONTEST. A STAR ATHLETE AT SAN FRANCISCO COLLEGE. HIS FIRST RECORDING... IN 1956 WAS "WONDERFUL, WONDERFUL" AND MADE JOHNNY AN IDOL OF MILLIONS OF TEEN-AGERS. IN LESS THAN TWO YEARS HE HAD ZOOMED TO A..... $100,000-A-YEAR SUCCESS! HIS SECOND AND THIRD - "IT'S NOT FOR ME TO SAY" AND "CHANCES ARE" PUT HIM IN THE MILLION-IN-SALES CLASS. BY 1974 THE GOLDEN VOICE OF THE INTERNATIONAL FAMOUS SINGER WHO ALWAYS SEEKS PERFECTION HAD 18-GOLD RECORDS AND 56-ALBUMS. ONE OF THE WEALTHIEST IN SHOW BUSINESS!

EASY!

Geo Lee

© 1977, George L. Lee Feature Service

ACTOR·PAINTER

BILLY DEE WILLIAMS

THE VERY TALENTED ACTOR WHOSE CAREER HAS BEEN A SERIES OF EXCELLENT PORTRAYALS ON STAGE, FILMS AND TV. BORN IN NYC A PRODUCT OF HARLEM ON APRIL 6, 1937. NAMED AFTER HIS FATHER, WILLIAM DECEMBER WILLIAMS. HIS FIRST ACTING EXPERIENCE AT 7 BY CHANCE. WHILE VISITING HIS MOTHER WHO WORKED AT THE LYCEUM THEATER, A PRODUCER WAS LOOKING FOR A YOUNG BLACK BOY... GAVE HIM A PART IN "THE FIREBRAND OF FLORENCE." BILLY ATTENDED THE HIGH SCHOOL OF MUSIC AND ART

BINGO LONG
MAHOGANY
SCOTT JOPLIN
HALLELUJAH BABY
I HAVE A DREAM
THE TAKE
THE COOL WORLD
A TASTE OF HONEY

BEAUTIFUL!

HE GAVE UP SERIOUS ART TO ACT BUT CONTINUES AS AN AMATEUR PAINTER.

BEFORE WINNING THE HALLGARTEN AWARD SCHOLARSHIP TO THE NATIONAL ACADEMY OF FINE ARTS AND DESIGN. HE STUDIED ACTING UNDER SIDNEY POITIER AT THE ACTORS WORKSHOP IN HARLEM. FIRST OFF-BROADWAY PLAY "BLUE BOY IN BLACK". FIRST MOVIE "THE LAST ANGRY MAN". WON AN EMMY NOMINATION FOR "BRIAN'S SONG". "LADY SINGS THE BLUES" CATAPULTED HIM INTO STARDOM!

ROLAND BURRIS

HIGHEST RANKING BLACK ELECTED OFFICIAL IN THE STATE OF ILL. THE FIRST BLACK TO BE ELECTED COMPTROLLER OF ILLINOIS (1978). RE-ELECTED IN 1982. BORN IN CENTRALIA, ILL. IN 1937 AND GREW-UP THERE. A GRADUATE OF SOUTHERN ILL. U., WITH A POLITICAL SCIENCE DEGREE (1959). STUDIED INTERNATIONAL LAW AS AN EXCHANGE STUDENT IN HAMBURG, GERM. ENTERED HOWARD U. LAW SCHOOL. GRADUATED 1963. BEGAN CAREER AS A NAT'L BANK EXAMINER WITH THE U.S. COMPTROLLER OF CURRENCY IN CHICAGO. JOINED CONTINENTAL ILL. NAT'L BANK AS A TAX

GEO LEE

IN 1982 HE WON RE-ELECTION WITH 2,327,779 VOTES-THE 3rd LARGEST TOTAL IN ILLINOIS HISTORY.' AS CHIEF FISCAL OFFICER HE CONTROLS A $17-BILLION BUDGET.' WOW.'

ACCOUNTANT (1964). IN 8-YEARS HE ROSE TO 2nd V. PRES. GOV. WALKER APPOINTED BURRIS DIRECTOR ILL., DEPT. OF GENERAL SERVICES (1973-77). IN 1984 HE RAN IN THE DEM. PRIMARY FOR THE U.S. SENATE. HE FINISHED SECOND IN A 4-MAN RACE. .. AFTER A FINE CAMPAIGN. BURRIS HAS SERVED AS PRES. OF THE NAT'L STATE COMPTROLLERS ASSOC. AND CHIEF FISCAL OFFICER OF PUSH.'

119

ATLANTA'S BLACK MAYOR

MAYNARD JACKSON JR

The First Black Man Ever to be elected Vice-Mayor of Atlanta, Georgia in its 122-year history, in 1969 at the age of 31. In 1973 he was elected Mayor and became the youngest Mayor of a major U.S. City...only 35. The Son of a Baptist Minister and a Grandson of John Wesley Dobbs one of Atlanta's First Families. He dropped out of the 10th Grade at 15 from Atlanta's Howard High to accept an early admisson scholarship to Morehouse College. He graduated at 18 and earned his Law Degree at No. Carolina Central U. Time Magazine named him one of the '200' Young Leaders of America in 1974. The Ebony Magazine named him among the '100' most influential Black Americans (1976-77-78).

GREATER RACE RELATIONS

LET THERE BE LIGHT

HIS LEADERSHIP WON HIM A SECOND TERM (1977)

A GREATER ATLANTA!

1979 GEO L. LEE FEATURE SERVICE

BIRMINGHAM'S BLACK MAYOR

DR. RICHARD ARRINGTON

Geo
LEE

ELECTED THE FIRST BLACK MAYOR OF ALABAMA'S LARGEST CITY ...BIRMINGHAM, ON OCT 30, 1979. A CITY COUNCILMAN FOR 8-YEARS. AN EDUCATOR, HE WAS ENCOURAGED TO RUN FOR MAYOR AND WON. BORN OF SHARECROPPER PARENTS IN LIVINGSTON, ALA., HE GREW UP IN FAIRFIELD, ALA. HIS EARLY EDUCATION IN THE PUBLIC SCHOOLS. ENTERED MILES COLLEGE, GRADUATED WITH A B.A. DEGREE IN BIOLOGY. EARNED HIS MASTER'S FROM THE UNIV., OF DETROIT AND HIS PH.D FROM THE UNIV., OF OKLAHOMA. STUDIED AT NEW MEXICO HIGHLANDS UNIV., STATE UNIV., OF IOWA AND HARVARD. AN OUTSTANDING STUDENT HE WON MANY HONORS. ONCE PROFESSOR OF BIOLOGY AND DEAN OF ACADEMICS AT MILES COLLEGE. DR. ARRINGTON WAS DIRECTOR OF THE ALABAMA CENTER FOR HIGHER EDUCATION WHEN HE RAN FOR MAYOR. HIS LEADERSHIP SHOULD BE GOOD FOR...BIRMINGHAM!

GIT OUTTA MA CITY

SHADES OF THE PAST!

I PLEDGE TO MAKE BIRMINGHAM A BETTER CITY!

"BULL" CONNOR CHIEF OF POLICE

MAYOR RICHARD ARRINGTON

HOPEFULLY...TIMES HAVE CHANGED

1981 GEO L. LEE FEATURE SERVICE

UNIVERSITY CHANCELLOR

DR. MARY F. BERRY

THE FIRST BLACK WOMAN TO HEAD A MAJOR U.S. UNIVERSITY ..."THE U OF COLORADO" IN 1976. STARTING FROM A SMALL COUNTRY SCHOOL NEAR NASHVILLE, TENN., SHE STUDIED HER WAY THRU HOWARD U. AND A PH.D IN HISTORY FROM U OF MICH (1966). WHEN PICKED FROM 300 CANDIDATES TO BE CHANCELLOR SHE WAS PROVOST OF BEHAVIORAL AND SOCIAL SCIENCES AT U OF MARYLAND!

MARY T. WASHINGTON

OF CHICAGO

FIRST BLACK WOMAN CPA (CERTIFIED PUBLIC ACCOUNTANT) IN THE U.S. (1939). STARTED HER CAREER AS A BOOKKEEPER FOR THE DOUGLAS NAT'L BANK (CHICAGO) AND LATER EARNED A BUSINESS DEGREE FROM NORTHWESTERN U. SHE IS SENIOR PARTNER OF HER ACCOUNTING FIRM. SERVED ON GOVERNOR'S AUDITING ADVISORY BOARD OF ILLINOIS (1963-65).

Geo LEE

1978 Geo L. Lee Feature Serv

D. C.'s DELEGATE TO CONGRESS

WALTER E. FAUNTROY

A SOUTHERN BAPTIST MINISTER BECAME THE FIRST MEMBER OF CONGRESS FROM THE DISTRICT OF COLUMBIA WHEN HE WON THE DISTRICT'S FIRST CONGRESSIONAL ELECTION SINCE 1872. HE WAS ELECTED IN MARCH 1971 TO THE NON-VOTING DELEGATE SEAT. A NATIVE OF WASH, D.C. HE BECAME INTERESTED IN THE NEW BETHEL BAPTIST CHURCH AND WANTED TO BE A MINISTER. HE ENTERED THE VIRGINIA UNION U., GRADUATING CUM LAUDE IN 1955... THEN TO YALE DIVINITY SCHOOL. AFTER GRADUATION, NEW BETHEL'S MINISTER DIED, THE CHURCH

SENT FOR YOUNG REV. FAUNTROY. HIS RETURN TO THE COMMUNITY WAS GOOD NEWS. DURING THE 1960s HE WORKED WITH DR. KING AND THE SCLC CIVIL RIGHTS MOVEMENT. REV. FAUNTROY HAS BEEN VERY ACTIVE IN HIS NEVER ENDING FIGHT FOR HUMAN RIGHTS! GOOD NEWS!

WALTER MARCHED WITH KING IN CHICAGO, 1965.

WHEN PRES. L.B.J. SIGNED THE VOTING RIGHTS ACT OF 1965, WALTER WAS THERE WITH KING.

1980 GEO L. LEE FEATURE SERVICE

"BENSON"

ROBERT GUILLAUME

STAR OF TV, STAGE, AND NIGHT CLUBS. THE LOVABLE BUTLER "BENSON" IN THE ABC SITCOM "SOAP," THE SPOOF OF DAYTIME DRAMA. HE STARTED IN 1977. HE PLAYED THE ROLE SO WELL HE WAS GIVEN HIS OWN SERIES..."BENSON" IN 1979 AND CONTINUES A HIT (1985). A SERIOUS ACTOR WHO PLAYS COMEDY VERY WELL. BORN IN ST.LOUIS, MO. AS A BOY HE LIKED SINGING AND IN HIGH SCHOOL TOOK PART IN MUSICALS. ENTERED ST. LOUIS UNIV., TO STUDY BUSINESS... BUT TRANSFERRED TO WASH. UNIV., FOR A MUSICAL CAREER. HIS VOICE TEACHER ENCOURAGED A CLASSICAL ONE. ROBERT WON A SCHOLARSHIP TO THE ASPEN MUSIC FESTIVAL IN COLORADO. BORN ROBERT WILLIAMS HE CHANGED HIS SURNAME TO GUILLAUME... APPEARED IN LOCAL MUSICALS IN CLEVELAND ...TOURED EUROPE, RETURNED...PLAYED "FINIAN'S RAINBOW" ON BROADWAY...TOURED WITH "PURLIE". IN 1976 WON A TONY NOMINATION... AS "NATHAN DETROIT" IN "GUYS AND DOLLS" ON BROADWAY. IN HIS EARLY YEARS HE SANG YIDDISH AND HEBREW TUNES IN NY'S ISRAELI NIGHT CLUBS. HIS MAIN INTEREST WAS IN CLASSICAL MUSIC... BUT THE MULTITALENTED GUILLAUME'S BIGGEST SUCCESS SEEMS TO BE TELEVISION.'

1985 GEO L. LEE FEATURE SERVICE

GUESS I'VE MADE IT!

A FEW CREDITS -- PURLIE 'JEFFERSONS
• KID FROM LEFT FIELD 'JULIA
• SEEMS LIKE OLD TIMES
• THE KID WITH THE 200 IQ

GUILLAUME WAS HONORED WITH HIS STAR ON THE FAMOUS WALK IN 1984.

HOLLYWOOD'S WALK OF FAME

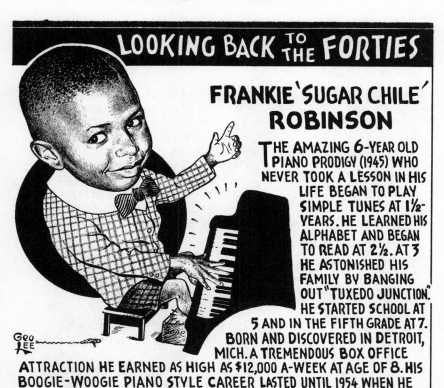

LOOKING BACK TO THE FORTIES

FRANKIE 'SUGAR CHILE' ROBINSON

THE AMAZING 6-YEAR OLD PIANO PRODIGY (1945) WHO NEVER TOOK A LESSON IN HIS LIFE BEGAN TO PLAY SIMPLE TUNES AT 1½-YEARS. HE LEARNED HIS ALPHABET AND BEGAN TO READ AT 2½. AT 3 HE ASTONISHED HIS FAMILY BY BANGING OUT "TUXEDO JUNCTION." HE STARTED SCHOOL AT 5 AND IN THE FIFTH GRADE AT 7. BORN AND DISCOVERED IN DETROIT, MICH. A TREMENDOUS BOX OFFICE ATTRACTION HE EARNED AS HIGH AS $12,000 A-WEEK AT AGE OF 8. HIS BOOGIE-WOOGIE PIANO STYLE CAREER LASTED UNTIL 1954 WHEN HE RETIRED. AFTER HIGH SCHOOL HE ENTERED OLIVET COLLEGE (MICH) IN 1957.

VALAIDA SNOW

WORLD-FAMOUS SINGING STAR AND TRUMPET PLAYER, SPENT 20-MONTHS IN A NAZI PRISON CAMP. SHE WAS FREED IN 1942. A GREAT VERSATILE STAR, SHE ONCE SANG IN RUSSIAN, HEBREW, ENGLISH AND PLAYED THE TRUMPET, VIOLIN, PIANO AND DRUMS IN A BROADWAY SHOW.

JULIAN BOND
OF ATLANTA, GA.

REP. OF THE GEORGIA STATE LEGISLATURE WAS THE **FIRST BLACK** AND THE **FIRST 28-YEAR OLD EVER PUT IN NOMINATION** AS **VICE-PRESIDENT OF THE U.S.** AT THE DEMOCRATIC CONVENTION IN CHICAGO-1968. A MOREHOUSE COLLEGE-DROP-**OUT WHO AS-PIRED TO BE A WRITER, START-ED HIS POLITICAL CAREER AS A SNCC CIVIL RIGHTS -**
SIT IN!

GEO LEE

LORRAINE
HANSBERRY
1930 - 1965

CHICAGO BORN PLAYWRIGHT WAS THE **FIRST BLACK WOMAN** TO HAVE A **PLAY** ON BROADWAY "A RAISIN IN THE SUN" THE FIRST WRITTEN BY A **BLACK,** TO RECEIVE THE **N.Y. DRAMA CRITICS CIRCLE AWARD** AS THE -**BEST PLAY** OF THE **YEAR** -1959.

SUPER FLY

CURTIS MAYFIELD

CREATIVE MESSAGE MUSIC GENIUS WAS BORN IN THE GHETTO ON CHICAGO'S WESTSIDE IN 1942. A VERSATILE SUPER STAR...GUITARIST, SINGER, SONG WRITER, ARRANGER, ACTOR AND BUSINESSMAN. HIS SCORE FOR THE MOVIE "SUPER FLY" (1972) GROSSED OVER 20-MILLION IN SALES FROM ALBUMS AND TAPES. HE STARTED HIS MUSIC ON AN OLD GUITAR AT AGE 9, LEARNING

GEO LEE

CURTIS HAS COMPOSED OVER 300 SONGS!

THE BASIC CHORDS. STARTED SINGING WITH THE NORTHERN JUBILEE SINGERS IN HIS GRANDMOTHER'S TRAVELING SOUL SPIRITUALIST CHURCH. AT 12 WROTE HIS FIRST SONG "GYPSY WOMAN", WHICH BECAME A HIT IN 1961 FOR THE SINGING GROUP-"IMPRESSIONS." AN ENTERTAINER FOR MANY YEARS. HE HEADS CURTOM RECORDS. WROTE MOVIE SCORES FOR...CLAUDINE, SPARKLE, SHORT EYES, LET'S DO IT AGAIN, A PIECE OF THE ACTION. CURTIS IS A BIG SUCCESS!

DIG THAT MUSIC

THAT'S SOUL

© 1978 GEO L. LEE FEATURE SERVICE

127

FAMED JAZZ GUITARIST

GEORGE BENSON

HIS GUITAR BRILLIANCE AND RANGE OF VERSATILITY AND A FINE VOCALIST HAS PUT HIM IN THE SUPERSTAR CLASS. BORN IN PITTSBURGH HE SHOWED THE FIRST SIGNS OF SHO-BIZ AT THE EARLY AGE OF 7. "LITTLE GEORGIE BENSON" SANG AND PLUCKED HIS UKELELE ON THE STREET CORNERS. AT 17 HE WAS WORKING CLUBS AS A VOCALIST-GUITARIST. WITH HIS OWN GROUP HE WENT TO HARLEM WHERE HE MET

FIRST GOLD RECORD, "BREEZIN" HAS SOLD 3-MILLION COPIES

"IN FLIGHT"

"WEEKEND IN L.A."

WON 3-GRAMMY'S IN 1976

"GIVE ME THE NIGHT"

GRAMMY AWARD

Geo LEE

"THIS MASQUERADE" BEST RECORD OF 1976

WON A CLIO AWARD FOR HIS RADIO COMMERCIAL "WEEKENDS WERE MADE FOR MICHELOB"

JOHN HAMMOND OF COLUMBIA RECORDS AND MADE HIS FIRST RECORDINGS (1966). BUT IT WASNT UNTIL 1975 WHEN HE SIGNED A MILLION-DOLLAR CONTRACT WITH WARNER BROS., AND BEGAN TO PLAY MELLOW POP SONGS ALONG WITH JAZZ... OVERNIGHT SUCCESS! HE MADE THE CONCERT TOUR, TV SHOWS, "LITTLE GEORGIE" HAS MADE IT-BIG!

1981 GEO L. LEE FEATURE SERVICE

KAREN STEVENSON

OF WASH, D.C., IS THE FIRST BLACK WOMAN TO WIN THE COVETED RHODES SCHOLARSHIP (1979) ONE OF THE HIGHEST HONORS FOR SCHOLASTIC EXCELLENCE IN THE WORLD. THE RHODES GIVES HER A 2-YEAR STUDY AT ENGLAND'S OXFORD U. A GRADUATE OF U. OF NO. CAROLINA AND A TOP TRACK STAR.

VINCENT BROOKS

A NATIVE OF FORT LEE, VA., IS THE FIRST BLACK BRIGADE COMMANDER AT THE U.S. MILITARY ACADEMY AT WEST POINT (1979) IN ITS 177 YEAR HISTORY. UNDER HIS COMMAND—THE ENTIRE BRIGADE OF-4,338 CADETS AND THE 4 CADET REGIMENTS!

Geo LEE

MARY E. TILLER

OF KANSAS CITY WAS THE FIRST BLACK MAJOR AIRLINE HOSTESS ON THE TRANS WORLD AIRLINES (TWA) IN 1959. SHE TOOK A CHANCE ON A HOMETOWN NEWSPAPER AD...AND PASSED HER TESTS!

Index

Index